Regular routines

D0244215

372.21094

WITHDRAWN FROM STOCK

Evesham & Malvern Hills College
Library

26636

CREDITS

British Library Cataloguing-in-Publication Data
A catalogue record for this book is available from the British Library.

ISBN 0 439 98348 7

The right of Jean Evans to be identified as the author of this work has been asserted by her in accordance with the Copyright, Designs and Patents Act 1988.

All rights reserved. This book is sold subject to the condition that it shall not, by way of trade or otherwise, be lent, hired out or otherwise circulated without the publisher's prior consent in any form of binding or cover other than that in which it is published and without a similar condition, including this condition, being imposed upon the subsequent purchaser.

No part of this publication may be reproduced, stored in a retrieval system, or transmitted, in any form or by any means, electronic, mechanical, photocopying, recording or otherwise, without the prior permission of the publisher. This book remains copyright, although permission is granted to copy pages 69 to 80 for classroom distribution and use only in the school which has purchased the book and in accordance with the CLA licensing agreement. Photocopying permission is given only for purchasers and not for borrowers of books from any lending service.

ACKNOWLEDGEMENTS

The publishers gratefully acknowledge permission to reproduce the following copyright material:

Jean Evans for 'The story of Holi', 'Jamie's story', 'Meet my friends', All about five', 'Sensing rain' and 'Whose special day?' © 2002, Jean Evans, all previously unpublished.

Every effort has been made to trace copyright holders and the publishers apologize for any inadvertent omissions.

AUTHOR
Jean Evans

EDITOR
Jane Bishop

ASSISTANT EDITOR
Lesley Sudlow

SERIES DESIGNER
Lynne Joesbury

DESIGNER
Paul Roberts

ILLUSTRATIONS
Maureen Galvani

COVER PHOTOGRAPH
Martyn Chillmaid

Text © 2002 Jean Evans
© 2002 Scholastic Ltd
Designed using Adobe Pagemaker
Published by Scholastic Ltd, Villiers House,
Clarendon Avenue, Leamington Spa, Warwickshire CV32 5PR
Printed by Alden Group Ltd, Oxford
Visit our website at www.scholastic.co.uk

1 2 3 4 5 6 7 8 9 0   2 3 4 5 6 7 8 9 0 1

CONTENTS

EVESHAM COLLEGE
LIBRARY

CLASS NUMBER	372. 210941
ACCESSION NUMBER	26636

CONTENTS

Introduction

This book focuses on everyday routines in early years settings. It aims to provide early years practitioners with a range of practical activities and supporting photocopiable sheets to extend learning opportunities for children aged three to five years old. The ideas have been carefully planned to provide a balance across all six Areas of Learning in the early years curriculum. The activity ideas are arranged around the routines of arriving and leaving the group each day, circle time, snack time, outdoor play, tidy-up time and story time.

The ideas will develop the social skills of sharing and taking turns by helping to prepare and serve snacks and will raise awareness of print through self-registration on arrival and by choosing library books at home-time. They will help children to solve mathematical problems by sorting equipment during tidy-up time as well as extend their knowledge of the natural world while playing outdoors, observing changes in the weather and setting up a feeding station for visiting birds. Children will be able to develop their physical skills, both indoors and outdoors, by dramatizing stories, cleaning equipment and playing games with small apparatus; and use imaginations to invent stories of their own for story time

How to use this book

The activity chapters contain ten activities each with a learning objective taken from one of the six Areas of Learning prescribed in the *Curriculum Guidance for the Foundation Stage* (QCA). All the chapters contain at least one idea for each Area of Learning. The ideas suggested can be applied equally well to the documents on pre-school education published for Scotland, Wales and Northern Ireland.

The activity pages all follow the same format, listing a 'Learning objective' taken from a specific Early Learning Goal; recommended 'Group size' and 'Timing', which are only guidelines as practitioners should be flexible according to the needs of the children in the group; items required in 'What you need', 'Preparation' (where necessary) and 'What to do'.

'Support' and 'Extension' suggest practical ways of adapting the idea to meet the needs of younger or less able children, and extending it to challenge older or more able children.

'Home links' provides ways of involving parents and carers in the activity, and extending this by further activities at home. It also helps to establish links between home and the setting. Whenever parents are mentioned, these comments are also intended to include carers and close family members involved in the children's lives.

The early years curriculum requires children to have a developing respect for their own cultures and beliefs and those of other people. The 'Multicultural links' suggested for many of the activities aim to raise the children's awareness of other countries, cultures, festivals and traditions.

Using the photocopiable pages

There are 12 photocopiable pages in this book, which aim to support or extend the individual activities, and these include stories, poems and matching cards as well as a song, recipe and game. The pages are valuable resources and are not intended to be used as time fillers, out of context. There are two new stories in the book, 'The story of Holi' on page 69, which provides a traditional tale from another culture, and 'Jamie's story' on page 70, a new fictional story to encourage children to use their own imaginative ideas to invent stories of their own.

There are three pages of new rhymes written to link closely to the activities and to extend children's learning. 'Meet my friends' on page 71 develops children's social skills, 'All about five' on page 72 increases counting skills, and 'Sensing rain' on page 73 raises children's sensory awareness. All the children will enjoy singing 'Whose special day?' on page 74 as part of birthday celebrations for their friends.

Activity sheets provide opportunities to work with adults to develop key skills in extending the main activities or to take home and share with parents and carers. The importance of forming links with parents and carers is stressed throughout the book and a recipe sheet is included on page 76 so that the children can continue the pizza-making activity at home, while the poem 'Welcome to our library' on page 75 encourages parents and carers to borrow books to share with their children at home.

Using resources

As the activities in the book involve daily routines, many of the resources are everyday items such as kitchen utensils and cleaning tools. The importance of these items is apparent throughout the book, perhaps most significantly when promoting mathematical skills. The resources mentioned should all be available within any early years environment, or otherwise easily obtained.

Many of the activities involve making cards, such as name cards and labels. A laminator is a useful accessory for creating strong, durable resources such as these. However, if you do not have access to a laminator, use sticky-backed plastic to protect the surface of the card.

The importance of how resources are organized is stressed in many of the chapters, and particularly when referring to tidying-up activities. Purchase strong plastic containers in attractive colours and consider matching the colour of containers to the resources they contain, for example, plastic construction equipment can be stored separately in small containers, one for each colour.

Create shadow templates where possible, for example, in sand, water and woodwork areas, so that the children can find what they need and return things to their designated places after use. Instructions are given for creating these templates in 'Room for one more?' on page 51.

Displays

A lot of the activities involve creating interactive wall and table-top displays for children to explore. It is important to present the children with attractive displays by using brightly-coloured backing papers and finishing them off with neat borders. Consider typing out captions on a computer and printing them in colours to contrast with backing papers or to link with the subject matter, such as 'autumn' or 'cold weather'.

Always keep displays tidy and replenish any resources that the children use. When purchasing resources, consideration should be given to including appropriate materials to create these attractive displays and maintain them. Ensure that staff know how to make full use of any technological resources by providing appropriate training.

Links with home

Developing close links between the children's home environment and that of the setting is extremely important, and routines are an ideal way to establish these links. From a purely practical point of view, parents are always closely involved with the routines of arriving and departing, and activities in this book suggest how to extend their involvement beyond the practicalities of finding clothes and belongings.

Do not confine this involvement simply to the entrance hall but invite parents and carers into your group to join the children at play, or to help staff with some of the routine organization, including the maintenance and preparation of resources. Always try to encourage parents and carers to help with activities, for example, outdoor games and visits. Suggest that they come and share any relevant experiences with the children during circle time and read stories to them at story time.

Send home regular letters and notices explaining your activities. Many of the photocopiable sheets in this book, such as rhymes and stories, can be sent home so that they can be shared with families.

Snacks and mealtimes are familiar social events to children, both in a home and group setting. Explain to parent and carers about your activities related to these times and suggest ways in which they can try similar activities at home. Invite parents and carers to come and prepare snacks with interesting new tastes from their own culture, whenever practicable.

Active learning

Familiarity with routines develops children's self-confidence and encourages them to see themselves as capable individuals who can make relationships, care for their own needs and have intellectual independence. Many of the activities in this book encourage children to become decision makers and problem solvers through regular routines. The activity, 'What would you like to do?' on page 25, for example, uses circle time as an opportunity for children to plan their own choice of activities. After enjoying the activities of their choice they then meet together again to review their actions. Building on what they can do and involving children in their own active learning is the basis of the 'plan, do and review' High/Scope approach. For more information about the High/Scope Principle contact: High/Scope UK, 192 Maple Road, London SE20 8HT. Telephone 020-8676 0220.

Equal opportunities

Every child has a right to develop and learn in an environment that is free from prejudice and discrimination, and all those involved with the group should work together in ensuring that meeting the needs of individuals underpins their approach at all times. Children who have special educational needs should be given appropriate facilities, and activities should be planned to include every child. All the activity pages contain ideas for supporting and extending activities to suit the children's different developmental stages.

CHAPTER 1

Use the children's arrivals and departures to provide interesting learning experiences including examining the group's resources and developing a sense of belonging through shared displays.

Welcome and goodbye

WHAT IS HAPPENING TODAY?

Learning objective
To continue to be interested, excited and motivated to learn. (Personal, social and emotional development)

What you need
Attractive resources from one of the activities for the session (such as bright tissue paper and string); photographs of the children working in regular play areas; card; thick pens; small table; bright table-cloth.

Preparation
Prepare a series of A4 cards, one for each play area, with an appropriate photograph at the top and a simple written explanation about some of the learning that might take place in that area. Mount these on a wall in the entrance area with the heading 'What can we do today?'. Prepare a thick sheet of card with two slots so that a caption about one of the main activities can be written on a strip of card and slotted through it. Write above the slot 'Today we will be' and below the slot 'We will be using some of the things on the table to do this. Pick them up and talk about them. We hope you will try our activity'.

What to do
Put the table under the wall display, cover it with the table-cloth and then stand the sheet of card prepared beforehand at the back. Slot a strip of card into it naming the main activity for the session, for example, 'Making kites'. Encourage parents and carers to go to the table as they arrive each day and to talk to their child about the objects that they see, drawing their attention to the wall display about regular play activities.

GROUP SIZE

Individual children with their parents.

TIMING

Ten minutes.

HOME LINKS

Send home a letter inviting parents to spend time reading the wall display and suggesting that they motivate their children by sharing enthusiasm for what is on offer each day.

MULTICULTURAL LINKS

Ensure that the captions on the display are in all relevant languages. If possible, invite bilingual parents to help with this.

Support
Make a staff member available to talk to younger children and their parents about the items on display. This will help to stimulate their interest and curiosity before they enter the setting.

Extension
Challenge older children and encourage their curiosity with a 'mystery object' table. Invite them to say what they think the main activity is going to be from the objects on display. Modify the card to read 'Can you guess what we will be doing with these things today?'.

WE ARE HERE

Learning objectives

To read a range of familiar and common words. (Communication, language and literacy)

What you need

Card; small pictures of everyday objects such as a flower, cat and teddy; computer; printer; laminator or sticky-backed plastic; hole-punch; string; brown and blue frieze paper; shiny red paper; brown collage scraps; green tissue; plastic hooks; plastic container.

Preparation

Use a computer to prepare a name card for each child and print the names out. Cut the card into rectangles, large enough for a child's name and a small picture. Invite each child to choose a picture to stick to one end of their card. Glue their name alongside and laminate or cover it in sticky-backed plastic. Punch a hole in the end of the card and attach a loop of string.

What to do

At circle time, hold up the name cards in turn and invite the children to each identify their own names.

Choose four children to help to make a large picture of a tree to display near the entrance. Back a display board with blue frieze paper and attach the outline of a tree made from brown paper. Invite the children to create leaves from green tissue paper and to add texture to the tree trunk with brown collage scraps. Cut out some apples from shiny red paper and ask the children to glue these to the tree. Glue plastic hooks to the apples.

Before each session, arrange the name cards on a table and ask the children to each find their card and hang it on one of the apples on the tree as they arrive. If the group is large, several cards can be hung on each apple. As they leave each day, ask the children to find their own cards, remove them and put them in a container.

Support

Younger children will be able to recognize their cards by the pictures at first. Draw their attention to the initial letters of their names.

Extension

Cut the pictures off older children's cards so that they begin to recognize their names by the letters alone.

GROUP SIZE
Individual children on arrival; six children for the counting activity.

TIMING
20 minutes.

COUNT THE BEARS

Learning objectives
To say and use number names in familiar contexts; to count reliably up to 10 everyday objects. (Mathematical development)

What you need
Small plastic bears; container; small doll's house; card; felt-tipped pens; balance pan.

Preparation
Create a chart with five columns, one for each day of the week, from Monday to Friday, divided into numbered squares. Provide enough squares for the number of children on the register for each session.

What to do
Leave a container full of plastic bears of the same size near the entrance of your setting and stand the doll's house alongside. Explain to the children that the doll's house is where the bears like to play. Ask them to take a bear from the container as they arrive and put it into the house to play.

When all the children have arrived, take a small group of children to the doll's house and ask them if they can tell you how many bears are playing there today. Count the bears together and put a tick in the correct square on the chart for that day. Repeat this daily for one week with different groups of children.

At the end of the week look at the chart together. Can the children tell you how many bears were playing each day? Which day had the most bears playing? Did any days have the same number of bears?

Count how many bears played on Monday and then count the corresponding number of plastic bears into a balance pan. Repeat this with Tuesday using the other pan. Can the children tell which pan has the most bears? Introduce the words 'balance', 'same', 'more' and 'less'.

Support
Younger children will enjoy simply transferring the bears from the container to play in the doll's house and counting them later. Simplify the activity by asking them to count the plastic bears in just one room of the house.

Extension
Present older children with simple problems involving counting bears or squares on the chart to compare daily attendance.

HOME LINKS
Encourage parents to count toys with their children as they tidy up and to involve them in counting cutlery as they set the table together at home.

MULTICULTURAL LINKS
Ask bilingual children to count the bears in their own language while the others listen.

GROUP SIZE
Four children to prepare the recycling containers; individual children to use them.

TIMING
20 minutes.

BRING IN YOUR TREASURE

Learning objective
To find out about their environment and talk about those features they like and dislike. (Knowledge and understanding of the world)

What you need
Four different-sized plastic containers; old greetings cards; sheets of card; sticky tape; glue; newspaper and magazine; recyclable materials such as cardboard tubes and yoghurt pots; small scraps of fabric.

What to do
Invite four children to help you to prepare the containers for recycling products. Give each child a sheet of card and provide one child with some old greetings cards, another child with a newspaper and a magazine, another with some scraps of fabric, and the fourth child with some recyclable materials such as cardboard tubes and yoghurt pots. Ask the first three children to cut out small pieces from their fabric and to glue these on to their cards to form a collage. Invite the fourth child to glue some of the recyclable materials on to the card. Create captions for each of the four types of recycled products, for example, 'Put your old cards in here'. Tape one of the children's collage cards along with the appropriate caption to the side of each container.

Ask the children to help you to decide where to put the containers so that they can easily be seen by parents and children on arrival. Make a large sign: 'Our recycling area' and display this above the containers.

At circle time, talk to the children about the importance of recycling materials and discuss what they do with unwanted items at home. Invite them to bring things from home to recycle into the four containers. Add more containers if you are collecting for a particular topic, for example, to hold leaves or shells.

HOME LINKS
Invite parents to encourage their children to bring things to your recycling area. Suggest that they take their children with them to local newspaper, can and bottle banks.

MULTICULTURAL LINKS
Display signs in different languages above the containers, if necessary, so that all parents can be involved in the activity.

Support
Help very young children to stick whole cards to the backing card rather than cut them into smaller pieces, and suggest that they tear the newspaper into pieces.

Extension
Invite older children to write or type the captions for the containers. Take them to visit a local recycling bank.

GROUP SIZE
Four children to
create the display;
individuals to use it.

TIMING
20 minutes.

WELCOME EVERYONE

Learning objective
To handle tools, objects and construction materials safely and with increasing control. (Physical development)

What you need
The photocopiable sheet on page 71; camera with film; coloured card; brightly-coloured frieze paper; paint; sponge shapes; double-sided sticky tape; ribbon; scissors; computer; printer.

Preparation
Take a photograph of each child and staff member beforehand and have the film developed. Use the coloured card to cut out a blank greetings card and attach a photograph inside each one so that the card stands up horizontally with the fold along the top. In your entrance area, back a low display board with brightly-coloured frieze paper. Type the children's names on the computer, print them and cut around them. Glue the names to the top of the cards containing the children's photographs with the fold of the card at the top. Attach a small piece of ribbon to this edge of the card so that the cards can be lifted when they are hanging on the wall.

What to do
At circle time, read the rhyme on the photocopiable sheet, 'Meet my friends', about belonging to a group. Talk with the children about your own group and what makes it so special. Suggest that you hang up photographs of everyone in the entrance area for visitors to see.

Ask a small group of children to use the sponge shapes to print designs all over the frieze paper on the display. Staple the prepared individual cards to the display by the back so that the front of the card forms a flap that can be lifted up to reveal the photograph underneath. Space the cards evenly. Add a title to the display 'Welcome to (name of your group)'. Invite the children to explore the display freely with their parents as they arrive each day. Suggest that they try to read the names on the tops of the cards before lifting the ribbons to see if they were correct.

Support
Put very young children's photographs alongside their names on top of the cards and ask parents for another photograph to put underneath.

Extension
Involve older children in taking the photographs, mounting them on the cards and typing and printing their names.

HOME LINKS
Ask parents for
baby photographs
of the children and
put these on top of
the cards instead of
their names. Add
the caption, 'Who
are these babies?'.

GROUP SIZE
Up to six children at a time.

TIMING
20 minutes.

LOOK AT US!

Learning objective

To explore colour, texture, shape, form and space in two and three dimensions. (Creative development)

What you need

The photocopiable sheet on page 71; safety mirrors; paper in various skin tones; selection of paint colours; paintbrushes; aprons; bright backing paper; contrasting-coloured frieze paper; border roll.

Preparation

In your entrance area, prepare a display board by backing it in the chosen frieze paper and adding a contrasting border.

What to do

Read the poem 'Meet my friends' on the photocopiable sheet and talk to the children about their own friends. Discuss the importance of belonging to a group and decide what makes your group special. What do the children like best about coming to the group? Suggest that it might be a good idea to paint pictures of everyone so that visitors can see all their happy, smiling faces when they come into the building and as they leave.

Supply the children with a good selection of colours and ask them to paint pictures of their own faces. Explain that this is called a 'self-portrait'. Encourage them to begin by looking in a safety mirror at their features. Talk about eye, hair and skin colour and any individual items such as hair bobbles. Encourage the children to respect differences by making positive comments, for example, about skin colour. Explain why some children need to wear things to help them to see or hear, such as spectacles or hearing aids.

Mount the children's portraits on backing paper and attach them to the frieze paper on the display board. Add the children's names underneath each portrait using clear lettering. Add a title to the display: 'Welcome to (name of group)'.

Support

Ensure that younger children are given large pieces of paper and brushes of a suitable size for their small hands. Give them plenty of praise for their attempts and talk to them about what they are doing.

Extension

Ask older children to paint pictures of staff members to add to the display. Encourage them to type or write their own names.

HOME LINKS
Encourage parents and carers to spend time discussing the display with their children on arrival or departure.

MULTICULTURAL LINKS
Supply paper and paint in a range of skin colours so that all children can create accurate likenesses of themselves.

Four children to create display; individual children to use it.

20 minutes.

CELEBRATIONS

Learning objective
To begin to know about their own cultures and beliefs and those of other people. (Knowledge and understanding of the world)

What you need
Brightly-coloured backing paper; card; scissors; streamers; greetings cards; wrapping paper; small boxes; paper; felt-tipped pens.

Preparation
Back a display board in the entrance area with brightly-coloured paper. Prepare a sheet of card with the caption, 'Today we are celebrating', written at the top and two slots at the bottom to allow a strip of card to be inserted. Attach the card to the backing paper in the centre of the display board.

> ### Today we are celebrating:
>
> Tom's birthday

What to do
Show the children the greetings cards, streamers and wrapping paper and talk about when they would see these items. Discuss celebrations in their lives and the lives of their families such as birthdays, Christmas, Divali, weddings and baptisms. Ask the children to draw a picture of a recent celebration using the felt-tipped pens. Write appropriate captions on the pictures for the children.

Mount the children's pictures on brightly-coloured paper to contrast with the colour on the display board, and attach them around the white card in the centre of the display. Ask the children to wrap up some small boxes into parcels with the wrapping paper and then to help you decorate the spaces on the display board with parcels, greetings cards and streamers.

At the end of each week, consider which celebrations such as birthdays and festivals will fall the following week. Write these on strips of white card, for example, 'Tom's birthday', 'the festival of Holi' and so on. Insert the cards into the slots on the display board at the start of each day.

Support
Use props such as imitation birthday cakes and parcels to stimulate younger children's memories of their family celebrations.

Extension
Encourage older children to write or copy their own captions under their pictures.

Encourage parents and carers to read the display board and talk to their children about the celebrations. Ask them to inform you of forthcoming family events such as weddings and baptisms.

Find out how different cultures celebrate and introduce some festivals to the children that you have not previously celebrated.

GROUP SIZE
Individual children
with parents on
arrival; up to 12
children at circle
time.

TIMING
Ten minutes.

WHAT IS THIS?

Learning objective
To be confident to try new activities, initiate ideas and speak in a familiar group. (Personal, social and emotional development)

What you need
Small table; card; unusual object such as a snowstorm in a plastic bubble, a piece of wood with a strange shape or an interesting holiday souvenir; magnifying glass.

Preparation
Create a stand-up sign from card with the caption, 'What am I? Look closely at me. Touch me and feel me'. Stand the card on a small table in the entrance hall alongside the unusual object. Include a magnifying glass for closer observations.

What to do
At circle time ask the children whether they noticed anything different as they came in at the start of the session. Can any of the children describe the unusual object? Did they use the magnifying glass to explore the object? What did they notice when they did this?

Hold up the object for the children to see and then pass it around the circle. Ask each child to think of something different to say about it. Encourage them to consider what it looks like, how it feels and whether it has a smell. Once the object has been passed around, extend the discussion further. A holiday souvenir could introduce a description of a holiday, or a small toy might lead to a story that you have invented.

Suggest to the children that they take turns to bring in an unusual object from home for the table. Each day invite a different child to talk about the object they have brought in.

HOME LINKS
Ask parents to
supply an interesting
object from home
and to come and
talk about it at circle
time.

Support
Help younger children to talk about the object by asking appropriate questions using familiar vocabulary, for example, 'Do you think it feels soft and cuddly?'. Praise them for their responses to develop their confidence when speaking in front of a group.

**MULTICULTURAL
LINKS**
Include interesting
objects associated
with a range of
cultures.

Extension
Ask older children to draw the objects and help them to write down their comments to make a home-made book.

GROUP SIZE
Four older children to help to set up the library area; individual children with parents.

TIMING
30 minutes.

LENDING LIBRARY

Learning objective

To show an understanding of the elements of stories and how information can be found in non-fiction texts. (Communication, language and literacy)

What you need

The photocopiable sheet on page 75; card; scissors; glue stick; box for tickets; book shelves or hanging rack; small table; pot plant; posters about reading and books; large and small chairs; selection of appropriate fiction and non-fiction books.

Preparation

Cut out some tickets from the card and create card pockets in each book to slot them into.

What to do

Talk to the children about sharing and enjoying books and suggest setting up a lending library in your group. Plan a visit to a local library to find out what you will need and ask the children to help you to make a list of the type of books and resources that they think should be included in your own library.

On return to your setting, explore possible sites for your library. If there is sufficient space, set up a permanent area near the entrance where parents can help their children exchange books independently. Ensure that the area is inviting by adding a pot plant on a small table, posters on the walls and comfortable seating so that parents and children can spend time choosing books together. Where space is limited, create a lending system on a trolley with a series of storage containers.

Involve small groups of children in role-play in the area so that they understand the process of exchanging books. Hang up notices explaining to parents how the library is organized.

HOME LINKS
Ask for parent volunteers to help with the organization of the library on a rota basis. Send home copies of the photocopiable sheet on page 75 and encourage parents to share and enjoy books with their children.

Support

Ensure that the library selection includes simple picture books with little text for younger children. Put up a recommended list of books for different ages so that parents can help their children to choose appropriate titles.

Extension

Have a section of books related to the children's growing interest in the world around them and the topics that you are covering.

MULTICULTURAL LINKS
Ensure that the books in your library represent a variety of different cultures.

GROUP SIZE
Six children.

TIMING
20 minutes.

1 to 2 children examining items that they have each placed in their own storage trays.

SECRET PLACES

Learning objective
To have a developing awareness of their own needs, views and feelings and be sensitive to the needs, views and feelings of others. (Personal, social and emotional development)

What you need
A storage trolley with a series of trays or strong stacking plastic paper trays; small pictures; card; computer; printer; peel-off labels; several personal items; small collage materials such as sequins and buttons; sticky tape.

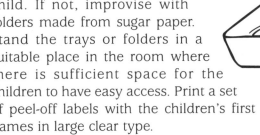

Preparation
Ensure that you have an individual storage tray for each child. If not, improvise with folders made from sugar paper. Stand the trays or folders in a suitable place in the room where there is sufficient space for the children to have easy access. Print a set of peel-off labels with the children's first names in large clear type.

What to do
Show the children some examples of personal belongings such as a small toy, a drawing and a pair of gloves. Talk about how these things are special to someone in the room and ask the children about their own special belongings. Suggest that it might be a good idea to have a private place to keep such things and show the children the storage trays that you have organized. Ask how you can make sure that the children know which trays belong to which child and invite them to make personalized labels for their trays.

Present the children with a strip of card cut to an appropriate size with a printed name label in the centre. Ask them to choose the collage materials freely to stick around their name label. Attach the finished strips of card securely to the trays with tape.

Talk to the children about what to store in their trays and encourage them to respect the privacy that these trays provide. Explain that they should not take things out of someone else's tray and reassure them that no one should take anything from theirs. Discuss taking the contents of the tray home at the end of each session.

Support
Invite younger children to choose a small picture to glue to their strip of card to assist identification.

Extension
Help older children to type and print out their own name labels.

HOME LINKS
Encourage parents to provide private places for children's secret belongings at home. Ask them to check the children's trays with them at the end of each session for the things that they have collected.

CHAPTER 2

Circle time

The shared experience of circle time provides the opportunity to extend children's enjoyment of personal and group celebrations and to encourage them to explore and respect cultural differences.

GROUP SIZE
Up to 12 children.

TIMING
Ten minutes.

HOME LINKS
Ask parents to supply old greetings cards to cut up.

MULTICULTURAL LINKS
Invite a parent to join circle time and talk about birthday traditions in their culture.

HAPPY BIRTHDAY TO YOU!

Learning objective
To respond to significant experiences, showing a range of feelings when appropriate. (Personal, social and emotional development)

What you need
The photocopiable sheet on page 74; small table and chair; ribbons; plastic flowers; card; small collage materials; glue; shoebox; birthday wrapping paper; strong square box; plaster of Paris; candles; candleholders.

Preparation
Work with a small group of older children to create a selection of home-made birthday cards covering the ages of the children in your group. Use small collage materials such as sequins, glitter and pictures cut from old birthday cards to decorate the cards. Put them in a shoebox covered in birthday wrapping paper. Decorate a small chair with ribbons and plastic flowers to become your 'birthday chair' and cover a strong box with plaster of Paris to create an 'iced birthday cake'. Create a chart depicting the birthdays of all the children and staff in your group and hang it on the wall for reference.

What to do
Just before circle time, on a day when a birthday arises in your group, put out the birthday chair with the imitation birthday cake and the box of cards on a small table in front. Push the appropriate number of candleholders into the cake and add the candles.

Towards the end of circle time, ask whether any of the children have a birthday today. Sing the first verse of the song 'Whose special day?' on page 74 and invite the appropriate child to sit in the chair while you sing the next verse. After the third verse, stop and ask the child's age and give the correct numbers of claps together. After the fourth verse, sing the child's favourite song together. Carefully light the candles and ask the child to blow them out before choosing a birthday card from the box and rejoining the others.

If a staff member has a birthday, hold the same ceremony and sing the song, but omit the verse about clapping their age!

Support
If younger children are uncomfortable about sitting in the chair, let them stay with the others or sit with a familiar staff member while you sing.

Extension
Invite older children to draw pictures and write small birthday messages in the cards.

GROUP SIZE
Up to ten children.

TIMING
20 minutes.

SHOW AND TELL

Learning objective
To speak clearly and audibly with confidence and control and show awareness of the listener. (Communication, language and literacy)

What you need
Items brought in by the children related to a particular theme such as 'summer', 'colours', 'toys' or 'holidays'.

Preparation
Send home a letter in advance explaining to parents that you would like their children to bring in something the following week related to the current theme, for example, a favourite toy or a pet accessory.

What to do
As the children arrive, ask them to put their chosen objects on a special table and explain to them that they can look at the objects but must leave them on the table as they are special to other children and could be damaged.

At circle time, arrange the table of objects nearby and ask a child to find their chosen object and return to the circle. Alternatively, put the objects within easy reach in the centre of the circle. Encourage the child to talk about the object, asking appropriate questions to develop confident use of language. Explain to the rest of the group about the importance of listening carefully and not interrupting, and remind the speaker to speak clearly so that everyone can hear.

When the first child has finished speaking, pass around the object and give each child the opportunity to handle it carefully and to think of something new to say about it. Emphasize that only the child holding the object should speak while the others listen. When the object has completed the circle, it can be returned to the table and the next child can repeat the activity.

Support
Encourage younger children to speak confidently in front of the group by making positive comments about their choice of object and asking appropriate questions to stimulate their thinking.

Extension
Extend older children's vocabulary by introducing alternative words and encouraging them to describe in more detail how their object looks, feels, sounds and smells.

HOME LINKS
Invite parents to bring in a relevant object of their own, such as an old toy or something related to a hobby. Ask them to join circle time to talk to the children about their chosen item.

MULTICULTURAL LINKS
Help those children who have English as an additional language by supplying them with some familiar words to describe their objects.

GROUP SIZE
GROUP SIZE
Up to 12 children.

TIMING
20 minutes.

To make salt dough
4 cups flour
2 cups salt
1 cup water
4 tablespoons oil
Mix the flour and salt, add the oil and gradually add the water to form a suitable consistency.

TAKE FIVE

Learning objective
To say and use number names in order in familiar contexts. (Mathematical development)

What you need
Three drawstring bags; felt or plain fabric; needle and cotton; salt dough; paint; props for the chosen number rhymes such as a small plastic frying pan, a green pencil case with zip, five plastic ducks, a baker's apron and some plastic coins.

Preparation
Cut out three large 'five' numerals from plain fabric or felt and sew one to the side of each drawstring bag. Type out the words to the children's favourite rhymes relating to the number five, stick these on to card and laminate. Put a rhyme into each bag. Prepare props for the chosen rhymes, using these ideas as a starting point:
• Use salt dough (see left) to create 'Five fat sausages'. Paint these pink and put them in a bag along with a small plastic frying pan.
• Make 'Five fat peas' from salt dough and paint them green. Put them inside a green pencil case and close the zip.
• Create 'Five currant buns' from salt dough (see left) with painted currants on top. Include five plastic coins and a baker's apron in the bag.

What to do
Show the children the 'number bags' and ask them what they notice. Choose a child to point to the number five on the side of each one. Decide which bag you will look inside and tip the contents into the centre of the circle. Can the children guess which rhyme they are going to sing? Read out the first verse on the rhyme card to see if they are correct. Sing the rhyme together, using the props to help you and invite the children to take part in appropriate actions. Put the items back in the bag and choose another one.

Additional ideas for rhymes can be found in *This Little Puffin...* compiled by Elizabeth Matterson (Puffin).

Support
Use rhymes involving two and three such as 'Baa Baa Black Sheep' or 'Two Little Dicky Birds'.

Extension
Create bags relating to the number ten such as 'Ten Green Bottles' or 'There Were Ten in the Bed' with older children.

HOME LINKS
Send home copies of the rhymes on the photocopiable sheet on page 72 for the children to share with their parents. Involve parents in creating the number bags and start a home loan scheme.

GROUP SIZE
Up to 12 children.

TIMING
20 minutes.

WHERE DOES IT COME FROM?

Learning objective

To begin to know about their own cultures and beliefs and those of other people. (Knowledge and understanding of the world)

What you need

Books, posters and artefacts relating to another country; an atlas or world map; an appropriate visitor; chair.

Preparation

Set up a table-top and wall display using the books, posters and artefacts to stimulate the children's interest beforehand. A wall display about China, for example, might contain posters of Chinese buildings and people, lanterns and fabric with a Chinese design. The table below might include examples of Chinese foods, a wok, chopsticks, rice bowls and a doll. Talk to the children who are exploring the display about what they can see and what they show an interest in.

Write or contact someone who has lived in, or visited, the chosen country and ask them if they would like to come to talk to the children and show them some interesting objects and photographs.

What to do

At the start of the discussion, ask the children whether they have noticed the display and what they can say about it. What did they like best about it? Do they know the name of the country where all of the things come from? Find it on a map. Tell them that they have a special visitor who has come to tell them more about the country.

Introduce the visitor and offer a chair. As the speaker is talking, note anything that the children might find difficult to understand and ask relevant questions to clarify these points.

Support

If younger children are uncomfortable in the company of a stranger, let them sit beside a familiar staff member. Keep the session short to retain their interest.

Extension

Involve older children in writing the invitation to the speaker and encourage them to make a book about the chosen country.

HOME LINKS
Send home a letter explaining to parents about the activity and inviting them to contribute to the display table. Ask if any parents could come to talk to the children about another country in the future.

MULTICULTURAL LINKS
Create displays about festivals and events from different cultures and invite parents and friends from the community to talk about how they celebrate the festival at home.

GROUP SIZE
12 children.

TIMING
20 minutes.

TRAP THAT BALL!

Learning objective
To use a range of small and large equipment. (Physical development)

What you need
A large ball; beanbags; quoits; rugby ball; beach ball.

What to do
Show the children the large ball and explain that you are going to demonstrate a game to play with it. Ask them to move back so that the circle becomes larger and then to open their legs wide so that their feet touch the feet of the children on either side.

Choose a child and say the child's name clearly before rolling the ball towards that child. The object of the game is for the children to grip the ball and 'catch it' as it rolls between their legs. Once the child has trapped the ball, then that child chooses someone else to roll the ball to and calls the relevant name. Vary the game, and encourage listening skills, by sometimes asking children to whisper the names very softly.

Develop physical skills further by considering other activities with small apparatus, for example, ask the children to throw and catch beanbags or pass quoits behind their backs around the circle. Have fun trying to roll a rugby ball, or a very large and light beach ball, across the circle.

Support
Simplify the game by letting younger children work in pairs. Ask each child in the circle to turn and sit facing a partner with their legs apart and feet touching so that they can have the satisfaction of successfully rolling the ball backwards and forwards. Once they become more skilled, they can move further apart.

Extension
Use a smaller ball and divide older children into two teams, wearing different-coloured bands, sitting alternately around the circle. They must then roll a ball to someone wearing the same colour. If the ball is not rolled accurately then someone from the other team might catch it instead. Until the children are ready for competitive play, do not count the points scored, simply encourage the children to enjoy the fun of the game.

HOME LINKS
Explain the learning objective of the activity and encourage parents to teach their children the ball games that they enjoyed playing when they were young.

MULTICULTURAL LINKS
Find out about games from other cultures and learn the rules to play with the children.

A WORLD OF MUSIC

Learning objective
To respond in a variety of ways to what they hear. (Creative development)

What you need
Music from different cultures (The Rough Guide to World Music CD has selections from a wide variety of cultures, for example, Volume 1 – Middle East, Europe and Africa; Volume 2 – Latin and North America, the Caribbean, India, Asia and the Pacific. Obtainable from The Festival Shop Ltd, telephone 0121-444-0444); tape recorder or CD player.

Preparation
Listen to the range of music available and choose appropriate selections. If necessary, record these on to a separate tape.

What to do
Ensure that the children have sufficient space between them so that they can concentrate without being disturbed. Tell them that you are going to play them some music and suggest that they close their eyes to listen. They can sit or lie on the floor so that they feel comfortable and relaxed.

Play the first extract of music and ask the children how they felt when they were listening. Did the music make them feel dreamy and sleepy or did they want to get up and dance or clap out the rhythm? What does the music make them think about?

Re-play the music and invite the children to respond to it by closing their eyes, clapping, tapping or moving to and fro.

Support
Do not expect very young children to be able to explain their feelings in too much detail. Support them by using vocabulary that they are familiar with and then introduce new words to encourage their verbal response, for example, 'You have a big smile after listening to the music, Kate. I think it made you feel happy because it was so lively'.

Extension
Talk to older children about where the music originated and show them examples or pictures of the instruments used. Let them try out some unusual instruments and comment on their origin and the sounds that they make.

GROUP SIZE
Six children.

TIMING
Ten minutes.

WHAT WOULD YOU LIKE TO DO?

Learning objective
To select and use activities and resources independently. (Personal, social and emotional development)

What you need
Photographs of the different play areas mounted on to card and protected with sticky-backed plastic or by laminating; an example of a resource from each of the different play areas such as a paintbrush or a sand scoop.

Preparation
Invite two children to help you to select a popular resource from each play area.

What to do
Develop the High/Scope Principle of 'plan, do and review' (see Introduction on page 8) by making this active learning part of your daily routine. In the early part of a session, ask a group of six children to sit in a circle with the photographs and resources in the centre. Invite each child to choose a photograph depicting the area that they would like to play in at some time during the session and to talk about what they plan to do in that area. Ask the same child to pick up the resource taken from that area and say how it could be used. When each child has planned, invite them to enjoy their chosen activities.

At the end of the session, work in small groups again, perhaps with key workers, talking about what the children have done and how their plans have worked out. Invite them to show the other children the things that they have created.

Support
Give younger children fewer choices and only use actual resources. Once they have chosen a resource representing a play area, suggest that they leave the circle and go to that area. If the area is already full, talk to the children about alternative play until a space in their chosen area becomes available.

Extension
Make a display board with photographs of the play areas and Velcro tabs underneath. Invite older children to attach small name cards to the Velcro tabs on two chosen activities. If there are no vacant tabs, explain that this means that the area is full initially, and they will need to choose another activity until a space becomes free.

HOME LINKS

Encourage parents and carers to involve the children in planning daily activities at home. For more information about the High/Scope Approach contact High/Scope UK, 192 Maple Road, London SE20 8HT. Tel: 0208 676 0220; fax: 0208 659 9938; email: highscope@btconnect. website: www.high-scope.org.uk

GROUP SIZE
Up to 12 children.

TIMING
15 minutes.

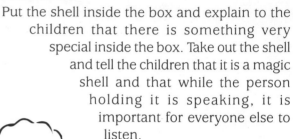

THE MAGIC SHELL

Learning objective

To sustain attentive listening, responding to what they have heard by relevant comments, questions or actions. (Communication, language and literacy)

What you need

A large shell or similar interesting object to pass around; attractive box to put it in.

What to do

Put the shell inside the box and explain to the children that there is something very special inside the box. Take out the shell and tell the children that it is a magic shell and that while the person holding it is speaking, it is important for everyone else to listen.

Hold the shell while you talk to the children about the importance of listening carefully to what others are saying, for example, when instructions are given. Ask how the children feel when they are trying to say something and another child begins to talk or does not listen.

Familiarize the children with the shell by passing it around and asking each child to say something about it. How does it feel? Hold it against one ear and describe the sound. What colour is it?

Once the shell has gone around the circle, invite a child to hold it while the others listen to that child's 'news'. When the child has finished, ask the others whether they would like to ask a question or say something about what has been said. If a child wishes to speak they should let you know by an agreed signal and the shell should then be passed across to that child.

Continue around the circle until all the children have held the shell and told the others their 'news'. Leave the shell on a low shelf so that the children can use it themselves during group discussions and role-play.

Support

Shorten the length of time to five minutes for younger children and let them just feel the shell if they do not wish to talk.

Extension

Play games to develop listening skills further such as 'Chinese Whispers' or 'Sound Lotto'.

HOME LINKS
Explain the significance of the magic shell to parents and send home suggestions to develop children's listening skills at home, for example, following simple instructions, listening to clapped rhythms and repeating them accurately or 'echoing' back words or phrases.

GROUP SIZE
Up to 12 children.

TIMING
15 minutes.

HOME LINKS
Hold a harvest festival and invite parents. Distribute harvest baskets to elderly residents in the locality.

MULTICULTURAL LINKS
Supply examples of fruits and vegetables from a range of cultures and find out how to prepare them.

HARVEST TIME

Learning objective
To begin to know about their own cultures and beliefs and those of other people. (Knowledge and understanding of the world)

What you need
Examples of local harvest produce such as an apple, a turnip and cabbage; produce from different countries such as a mango, sweet potato and pawpaw; two large pillowcases or drawstring bags.

Preparation
Put the local produce in one bag and the produce from other countries in the other. Check for any food allergies or dietary requirements among the children. Set up a display using examples of the items in the bags so that the children can explore them by touch, smell and appearance before the circle time activity. Label the items.

What to do
Begin by asking the children if they have explored some of the things on the harvest display and inviting them to talk about their discoveries. Explain the meaning of the word 'harvest'.

Hold up the bag containing the local harvest produce and ask the children what they think might be inside. Pass the bag to a child and invite that child to choose an object and describe how it feels. Can the child guess what it is or point to a similar item on the table display? Ask the child to pull the item out of the bag and see if the guess was correct. Name the item and ask the children to repeat the word. Have the children ever tasted it? Did they like it? Was it cooked or raw when they tasted it?

Choose children in turn and repeat the activity until the bag is empty. Return the produce to the bag and put the other bag in the centre of the circle. Repeat the activity, this time asking the children to describe the product but telling them the name and where it comes from. Arrange a tasting table to follow on from this part of the activity.

Support
Have one bag of familiar produce for very young children to guess and name.

Extension
Concentrate on products from other cultures with older children. Look at a world map to find the countries of origin.

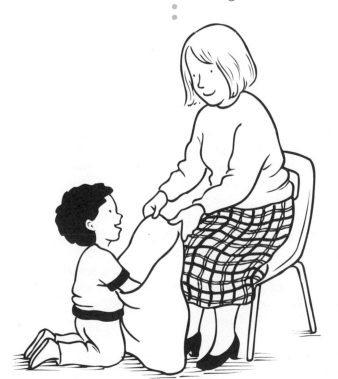

GROUP SIZE
Up to 12 children.

TIMING
Five minutes.

STORMY WEATHER

Learning objective
To look closely at similarities, differences, patterns and change. (Knowledge and understanding of the world)

What you need
Thick card; scissors; glue; computer; printer; paper; items associated with different weather conditions such as a small umbrella, sun-glasses and a woollen hat; three shallow plastic trays; storage container.

Preparation
Create a calendar by typing the names of the days and months, and numbers up to 31, in clear, bold type. Print these and mount them on strips of thick card. Make the calendar base from thick card and cut three sets of slots in it so that the strips can be inserted. Store the spare strips in separate trays. Put the collection of objects related to weather conditions in a storage container in the centre of the circle and prop the calendar on a low table nearby.

What to do
Begin by asking the children to tell you what day it is. Invite an older child to find the correct word in the appropriate tray and insert it into the calendar. Ask another child to help you to find the correct number for the date and the name of the month. When the calendar is completed read it together.

Talk about the weather. Was it warm or cold when the children arrived? What sort of clothes were they wearing? Compare weather conditions throughout the week and refer to seasonal changes. Invite younger children to help you to find appropriate objects related to the day's weather conditions in the container and to put these on to the table next to the calendar.

Support
Support younger children by talking about the things that they choose from the container. Initially, many children will simply choose things that they are attracted to. If the object is unsuitable suggest that you look out of the window together and consider, for example, how the child would feel going outside in a woollen hat on such a hot day.

Extension
Draw older children's attention to initial letter sounds to help them to identify the words on the cards.

HOME LINKS
Explain the activity to parents and ask them to talk to their children about changes in the weather when they are outdoors.

MULTICULTURAL LINKS
Talk about climate in other countries and make comparisons. Look at clothes worn by children from different cultures and discuss how these are influenced by the weather.

CHAPTER 3

Snacks and meals

Raise the children's enjoyment of snacks and meals through active participation with these activities which are all related to food. Be aware of any food allergies and special dietary requirements of individual children in your group and maintain strict rules for hygiene.

GROUP SIZE
Up to six children.

TIMING
15 minutes.

HOME LINKS
Explain to parents and carers how children are encouraged to help with routines to develop social skills and suggest that they involve their children with domestic routines at home.

MULTICULTURAL LINKS
Consider any special dietary requirements the children might have related to their cultures. Introduce food from other cultures at snack time.

HELP A FRIEND

Learning objective
To consider the consequences of their words and actions for themselves and for others. (Personal, social and emotional development)

What you need
Children's mugs and plates; jug; place mats; serviettes; snack food; drink.

Preparation
Before snack time, choose two older children from each small group to help to prepare the snack and to set the table for their group. Talk to them about the needs of the youngest children, for example, considering whether some food should be cut into smaller bite-sized pieces. Emphasize the importance of the older children's help in ensuring that snack time is healthy and safe for the younger children. Always check for allergies and dietary requirements when choosing foods.

What to do
Invite the children to sit in small groups for a snack. Organize 'family' groups by choosing a mixed-age range of children to sit with the same member of staff daily.

Provide named place mats (see 'Name that place' on page 30) and, if possible, arrange these so that younger children sit between older children. As the children find their seats encourage older ones to help their younger friends to find their places.

During snack time, ask staff members to develop conversation between the children and to involve older children in pouring out drinks for younger ones. Avoid unnecessary spills by only half-filling the jug and suggesting that the children only have half a cup at a time. Top up the jug as required. Ask older children to pass around plates of food such as chopped raw vegetables and fruit so that the other children can help themselves. Once the food has been eaten involve the older children in clearing away plates and mugs and wiping the tables.

Support
Encourage younger children to ask their older friends for support when they need it during other activities.

Extension
Talk to older children about how inappropriate actions such as snatching equipment can make others feel unhappy. Contrast this with talking about helping younger children at snack time to make them feel secure.

GROUP SIZE
Whole group discussion, then four children.

TIMING
Ten minutes.

NAME THAT PLACE

Learning objective
To link sounds to letters, naming and sounding the letters of the alphabet. (Communication, language and literacy)

What you need
A4 coloured card; early years and mail order catalogues; scissors; glue; small collage materials such as sequins and shiny paper; computer; printer; white paper; laminator.

What to do
At circle time, explain that you are going to help the children to make their own place mats so that they will know where to sit at snack time or mealtime. Discuss how they will know which mat is theirs. Hold up their name cards and talk to them about the initial letters and the sounds that they make. Talk about putting their initial letter on the place mat. Would that help? What if two children had names with the same initial letter? Suggest typing out their whole name instead. How will the younger children who cannot recognize their names yet know which is their place mat? Show them the catalogues and suggest that they find pictures of familiar things such as toys to stick on the mats to assist recognition.

In small groups, help the children to type their names using large clear lettering and print these out. Talk to them about the names of the letters and the sounds that they make. Cut around the children's printed names to form an oval shape and ask them to

glue these to the centre of a piece of coloured A4 card. Supply the children with catalogues and let them choose pictures to cut out and arrange around their names on the card. Fill in spaces with small collage materials such as shiny paper scraps and sequins. When the children are happy with the final design for their place mats, laminate them for protection.

Support
Prepare younger children's names for them and refer to the initial letter as they stick them to the cards. Help them to cut out pictures of their choice.

Extension
Encourage older children to type their names by themselves, copying from a name card, if necessary.

HOME LINKS
Let each child make an additional place mat so that they can take one home. Encourage parents to use the same lettering style as your setting when writing their child's name.

GROUP SIZE
Whole group
working in smaller
groups.

TIMING
Ten minutes.

ALL THE SAME?

Learning objective
To use language such as 'more' or 'less' to compare two numbers. (Mathematical development)

What you need
Small tables; cups; plates or small bowls; serviettes; snack ingredients such as apples and bananas; squash or juice; knife.

Preparation
Prepare for snack time beforehand with a group of children, for example, by cutting up fruit (leaving some whole as examples), spreading crackers, filling jugs and putting place mats on the tables (see 'Name that place' on page 30). Always check for allergies and dietary requirements when choosing foods.

What to do
Arrange everything on a low table so that the children have easy access. Ask them to find their place mats and sit down at small tables ready for a snack. Invite individual children to count how many are at their table and to come and collect the correct number of cups so that each child has one. Try to include appropriate vocabulary in the conversation while the children are counting out the cups by asking questions about whether 'more' or 'less' cups are needed and by how many. Repeat this with other children counting out bowls, plates and serviettes as appropriate.

Show the children the snack for the day, for example, a whole apple and banana, and talk about how you can be sure that each child has the same amount. Cut up the whole fruit after deciding on the approximate size of each slice and add these to the previously prepared fruit. Choose children to distribute the slices of fruit equally into the individual bowls.

Put a jug of the chosen drink (not too full) on each table and ask a child who has not already helped to pour this out into individual cups, emphasizing the need to try and make sure that everyone has a similar amount, again using appropriate vocabulary. Explain that water is available for any children who do not want the chosen drink.

Invite individual children to distribute any other snacks equally, such as crackers or vegetable sticks.

Support
Let younger children help older ones with counting, sharing and distributing.

Extension
Challenge older children by asking how many more cups are needed for six rather than four children.

HOME LINKS
Send home a sheet explaining to parents how they can encourage their children to use mathematical language at home by involving them in domestic routines such as setting tables and weighing baking ingredients.

BREADS AND SPREADS

Learning objective
To investigate objects and materials by using all of their senses as appropriate. (Knowledge and understanding of the world)

What you need
Various breads; soft cheese, jam and honey; spreadable butter; soft margarine; toaster; knives; forks; spoons; large and small plates; breadboards; bowls.

Preparation
Always check for allergies and dietary requirements when choosing foods. Cut the bread into individual portions and put samples of the spreads into bowls. Ensure that the children have washed their hands before starting the activity.

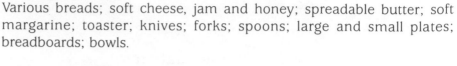

What to do
Arrange the bread varieties on separate large plates or breadboards in the centre of the table and ask a staff member to prepare some toast.

Begin by asking the children what they can see on the table. Do they know that they are all different types of bread? Can they point to some white bread and then some brown bread? Show them a more unusual bread such as ciabatta and talk about the country of origin. As you talk, give the children small samples of different breads and discuss texture, smell and taste. Compare a slice of bread before and after toasting.

Look closely at the different spreads and pass the bowls around for the children to smell the contents. Talk about whether the spreads look hard or soft. Show the children the knives, forks and spoons and decide which will be most suitable for applying the spreads to the breads. Invite the children to make their own snacks with the ingredients in front of them using tools of their choice. Encourage them to talk about their likes and dislikes and what they notice about smell, taste and texture.

Support
Give younger children less choice and a greater contrast, for example, brown and white bread and one sweet and one savoury spread. Make sure that the tools are safe and easy for them to handle, for example, sturdy plastic knives.

Extension
Involve older children in preparing sandwiches for the rest of the group. Encourage them to choose their own combinations of fillings and to serve the others at snack time.

GROUP SIZE
Four children.

TIMING
Ten minutes.

FILLING NOT SPILLING

Learning objective
To handle objects safely and with increasing control. (Physical development)

What you need
Water tray; jugs of various sizes; table; towel; aprons; children's mugs; water.

What to do
Ask the children to put on aprons. Take them to an empty water tray and explain that you have decided that you would like them to pour their own drinks out at snack time but that you are not sure which jugs to use to make the task easy for them. Show them the different-sized jugs arranged on a towel on a table nearby and ask them to arrange them in order of size. Which ones do they think would be easy to pour their drinks from, and which ones would be more difficult? Discuss reasons for their choices and suggest trying their ideas out in the empty water tray where it would not matter if there were lots of spills.

Fill the largest jug to the top and put it in the tray along with some children's mugs. Invite the children to take turns to try to fill a mug. Was this easy? Did they spill any water? Talk about why the task was difficult by referring to the amount of water and the size of jug. Try again with the jug half full. Was it easier this time?

Continue to fill and empty the mugs, using all of the jugs, until the children decide on the most suitable jug size and the amount of liquid to put in it. At snack time, present the children with the jug of their choice containing the chosen amount of liquid and ask them to pour out their own drinks. Discuss how well they managed the task and whether they will need to modify their choice before the next snack time.

Support
Do not give younger children full jugs that are too heavy to lift. Praise them for their actions and encourage them to try out different options.

Extension
Invite older children to prepare the drinks and pour them out for the very youngest children. Praise them for their developing skill.

HOME LINKS
Explain the activity to parents and suggest that they give their children plastic jugs and mugs to fill and empty at bathtime.

GROUP SIZE
Four children.

TIMING
20 minutes.

HOME LINKS
Send home a copy of the basic pizza recipe on the photocopiable sheet on page 76 for parents to make with their children.

MULTICULTURAL LINKS
Follow simple snack recipes from other cultures, seeking advice and suggestions from parents where available.

PIZZA FUN

Learning objective

To express and communicate their ideas, thoughts and feelings by using a widening range of materials, suitable tools and designing and making. (Creative development)

What you need

The photocopiable sheet on page 76; 300g self-raising flour; 80g butter; 100g grated cheese; eight tablespoons milk; two tins of tomatoes; two dessertspoons tomato purée; pizza toppings such as ham, grated cheese, sausage, mushroom, red, yellow, orange and green peppers, sweetcorn, tuna, pineapple; aprons; chopping boards; mixing bowls; rolling-pins; knives; teaspoons; wooden spoons; cheese grater; baking trays; scales.

Preparation

Grate some cheese and slice and chop up some red, yellow, orange and green peppers. Slice a sausage and cut some ham into strips. Display the pizza toppings in bowls. Always check for allergies and dietary requirements when choosing foods.

What to do

Ask the children to wash their hands and put on aprons. Give them a mixing bowl each and weigh out 75g self-raising flour and 20g butter into each one, encouraging all of the children to help you with measurements. Ask the children to rub the flour and butter together until their mixtures are crumbly. Let them take turns to grate 25g of cheese into each bowl along with two tablespoons of milk. Encourage the children to mix the ingredients with the wooden spoons until they have created a ball of dough. Ask them to roll out their dough balls into flat circles and put them on a baking tray. Make a tomato sauce from a tin of tomatoes, thickened with tomato purée, and invite the children to spread this on the top of their pizzas.

Give the children a selection of toppings to decorate their pizzas, then cook them in the oven at 220°C/425°F/Gas Mark 7 for approximately fifteen minutes. Let the children enjoy the pizzas at snack time.

Support

Help younger children to rub the flour and butter together and grate the cheese for them.

Extension

Encourage older children to consider the appearance of their finished pizza. They might like to create a pattern or a face from the toppings. Try not to make suggestions, but praise them for their individual ideas.

SLOW AND EASY

Learning objective
To recognize the importance of keeping healthy and those things that contribute to this. (Physical development)

What you need
Three eating apples; three bananas; crackers; soft bread; cheese spread; plates; knives.

Preparation
Always check for allergies and dietary requirements when choosing foods.

What to do
Give each child a plate, knife and half a banana and ask them to cut the banana into slices. Now give them a quarter of an apple with the pips removed and ask them to try to slice that as well. Which of the two fruits was easier to slice? Ask the children to name other fruits they enjoy eating and discuss the importance of eating fruit as part of a healthy diet.

Invite the children to eat the fruit that they have prepared. Does it take longer to chew up the apple or the banana? Can the children give reasons for their answers? Explain about the importance of chewing food properly, not talking while eating and not rushing meals and snacks.

Give each child a cracker and a piece of soft bread and ask them to put some cheese spread on them. Let the children eat these and talk again about which takes longest to chew and why. Extend the discussion to include talking about caring for teeth by eating appropriate foods and cleaning them regularly.

Once the children have finished their snack, explain to them that it is important to enjoy a calm activity after a meal or snack. Make it part of your routine to choose something quiet to do together at the end of snack time, for example, say some rhymes or discuss planned activities.

Support
Do not give very young children hard fruit or crackers to chew. Encourage them to become familiar with routines of eating quietly and then enjoying a quiet activity rather than giving them explanations at this stage.

Extension
Involve older children in choosing rhymes to sing at the end of snack time. Talk to them about the contribution that regular routines make towards a healthy lifestyle such as eating, sleeping and taking exercise.

GROUP SIZE
Two children at a time.

TIMING
Five minutes.

SNACK BAR

Learning objective
To select and use activities and resources independently. (Personal, social and emotional development)

What you need
Children's plates and mugs; jug; chosen snack food and drink; large plates; appropriate cutlery; serviettes; washing-up bowl and liquid; tea towel; three small tables; table-cloth; vase of flowers; card; scissors; laminator; felt-tipped pens; small pictures; two shoeboxes (one with a lid); wrapping paper with food design.

Preparation
Make some laminated name cards for the children with a picture on each one to assist recognition. Cover the boxes with wrapping paper and cut a slot in the lid of one of them, large enough to post the cards through. Put the cards in the other.

Set out an attractive snack area with a table-cloth and vase of flowers. Half-fill a jug with the chosen drink and put the snack on a plate covered with a clean serviette. Include the children's mugs, plates and any cutlery needed. Put the name-card boxes on a table alongside and arrange washing-up resources on another table. Always check for allergies and dietary requirements when choosing foods.

What to do
Explain to the children that they can visit the snack area when they feel ready for something to eat and drink, but that they should each make just one visit. Reassure them that they can have a drink of water whenever they wish to.

Show them how to use the area. Explain that they should find their name cards and post them in the shoebox so that staff know who has had a snack.

Demonstrate how much liquid to pour into a mug to avoid spillages and explain that the food is under the serviette to keep it free from germs. Tell them that sometimes there will be cutlery on the table so that they can apply spread or cut up fruit. Show them where to wash their plates and mugs afterwards.

Support
Make the process simple for younger children by preparing the snack beforehand and pouring out drinks.

Extension
Invite older children to take turns to be 'snack helpers' to keep the area tidy and replenish supplies.

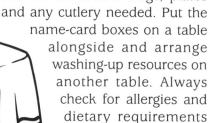

HOME LINKS
Explain to parents about the self-service system and encourage them to help their children to be more independent during mealtimes at home.

MULTICULTURAL LINKS
Consider children's individual cultural and religious differences when planning snacks and setting up this area.

GROUP SIZE
Four children.

TIMING
Ten minutes.

MATCH THAT PLACE

Learning objective
To use developing mathematical ideas and methods to solve practical problems. (Mathematical development)

What you need
Place mats (see 'Name that place' on page 30); cutlery; mugs; plates; serviettes.

What to do
Invite four children to be helpers. Depending on individual circumstances, the group can help to set tables for a snack or meal or, for sessional care groups, to set the table in the home area.

Put the appropriate number of chairs around a table beforehand, then talk to the children about how many children will sit at each table. How can they tell? Suggest that they decide by counting the chairs that you placed around the table. Ask each child to set a separate table if possible. Begin by putting out the place mats and continue to add items, counting out mugs, cutlery, plates and serviettes as you do so. For sessional care groups, work together to set a table for four toys in the home area.

Once all of the tables are set, present problems to the children by asking questions, for example, 'Is there a knife, fork and spoon at every place?'. Where appropriate, consider whether place settings match by colour, for example, 'Does every blue plate have a blue mug beside it?'. Decide if the cutlery and seating is suitable for any younger children at the table. Invent simple fictitious problems while you are busy. Suggest that a child suddenly has to go home early. What should be done about the place that the children have set? How many items will they need to take away? What would happen if a child arrived unexpectedly? What would be needed to create an additional place setting?

Support
Work with younger children as one group, setting one table and talking about what you are doing. Make place mats with templates for a plate, mug and cutlery so that they can match items to their appropriate places by shape and size.

Extension
Invite older children to complete the place setting on the photocopiable sheet by cutting out the items and sticking them in the appropriate place. Ask them to colour the items so that they match.

HOME LINKS
Give each child a copy of the photocopiable sheet on page 77 to complete at home. Ask parents to let their children help to set the table. Explain the learning objective so that they include mathematical language and ideas as they do so.

GROUP SIZE
Four children.

TIMING
Ten minutes.

SPLAT THOSE GERMS!

Learning objective
To dress and undress independently and manage their own personal hygiene. (Personal, social and emotional development)

What you need
Spot stickers; card; soap; paper-towels dispenser; bin.

Preparation
Divide a sheet of card into columns and write the names of the children in the columns along the top of the chart. Divide the columns into smaller squares. Write the caption 'I remembered to wash my hands' on a strip of card. Hang the chart on the wall in the cloakroom near to the hand basins, or alongside the washing facilities in the activity room, if appropriate. Attach the caption strip above it.

I remembered to wash my hands

	Jack	Rosie	Dan	Amy	Jo	Asif
5						
4				●		
3	●		●	●		
2	●	●	●	●		●
1	●	●	●	●	●	●

What to do
Talk to the children about the importance of washing their hands, for example, before eating and after painting or using the toilet. Take them into the cloakroom and show them how to use the facilities properly. Demonstrate how to flush the toilet and how to use the taps, soap and paper-towel dispenser and to dispose of the used towel in the bin. Ask the children to wash their hands while you watch and encourage them to do this thoroughly.

Show the children the chart on the wall and explain that it is there to record how many times they wash their hands during the session. Demonstrate how to peel off a sticker from a sheet and stick it into an appropriate square on the chart.

At the end of the session, look at the chart together and talk about when the children washed their hands and why. Praise them for their actions and their clean hands. Once the children are comfortable with the routine, remove the chart and reintroduce it at intervals to maintain their awareness.

Support
Encourage younger children to talk to you about when they have remembered to wash their hands rather than using the sticker system. Help them with the process initially until they can manage competently.

Extension
Extend explanations about reasons for hand washing to include information about germs and talk about other routines for caring for the body such as washing hair, bathing and cleaning teeth.

HOME LINKS
Invite parents to encourage their children to wash their hands as part of their daily routines at home. Ask them to ensure that there are appropriate facilities for them to manage independently, such as a step up to the basin and access to soap and a towel.

CHAPTER 4

Out to play

Develop the children's learning on a much larger scale by using the outdoor environment in all but the most severe weather conditions. Let the children explore the rain and wind and learn about protection from the sun with these activities.

GROUP SIZE
Four children.

TIMING
20 minutes.

PLAYING BY THE RULES

Learning objective
To understand what is right, and what is wrong, and why. (Personal, social and emotional development)

What you need
Large apparatus such as a climbing frame and slide); small apparatus such as balls and beanbags; clipboard; paper; pen; laminator; computer; printer.

Preparation
Arrange the apparatus in the outdoor area, or a large indoor space, leaving some equipment in a potentially dangerous position, for example, balls at the bottom of the slide steps.

What to do
Talk to the children about playing safely outdoors. Have they ever hurt themselves? How did the accident happen? Suggest that they help to arrange the equipment safely before the others go outside. Use the clipboard to write down things that you need to do to make sure that the children can play safely.

Go outdoors and walk around the area. Can the children see anything that might cause an accident? Prompt them with appropriate questions, for example, 'What could happen if someone stood on this ball as they tried to climb up the slide steps?'. Discuss whether it is a good idea to have large and small apparatus together and find ways of separating the two, for example, with a chalk line on the floor. Move apparatus until you are satisfied that there are no hazards.

Ask the children to consider how their behaviour affects safety. What could happen if someone pushed another child at the top of the slide or climbing frame? Is it a good idea to ride bikes and cars around climbing apparatus? Why not? Ask questions and write down safety decisions.

Go back indoors and read out your notes to the children. Reword these as simple rules. Type and print out the rules and laminate the sheet for reference during outdoor play.

Support
Reinforce simple safety rules as younger children play so that they become aware of the reasons for the boundaries that have been set.

Extension
Involve older children in making decisions about simple rules in play areas within the indoor environment.

HOME LINKS
Show parents the sheet of rules for outdoor play and ask them to talk to their children about safe behaviour, and the consequences of inappropriate actions.

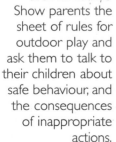

GROUP SIZE
Up to 12 children.

TIMING
15 minutes.

RING-A-RING O' ROSES

Learning objective

To listen with enjoyment, and respond to stories, songs and other music, rhymes and poems. (Communication, language and literacy)

What you need

Just the children and sufficient space (outdoors or indoors).

What to do

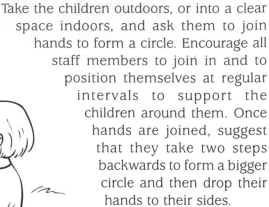

Take the children outdoors, or into a clear space indoors, and ask them to join hands to form a circle. Encourage all staff members to join in and to position themselves at regular intervals to support the children around them. Once hands are joined, suggest that they take two steps backwards to form a bigger circle and then drop their hands to their sides.

Develop the children's confidence by singing familiar nursery rhymes, such as 'Baa Baa Black Sheep', clapping the rhythm while standing still. Invite the children to request favourite rhymes.

Ask the children to hold hands again and enjoy simply walking around and saying rhymes in time to the children's strides. Once the children manage to walk around while singing, choose songs in which all of the children can follow the same actions such as 'Ring-a-ring o' Roses'. Gradually introduce more complex action songs involving the children taking different parts such as 'The Farmer's in His Dell' and 'There Was a Princess Long Ago' from *This Little Puffin...*, compiled by Elizabeth Matterson (Puffin).

Support

Arrange for older children and staff members to stand next to younger children to support them during the songs and games. If the youngest children are overwhelmed by bigger, boisterous children then let them play in a smaller group with a familiar staff member, or encourage them to watch until they feel ready to join in with confidence.

Extension

Introduce older children to more exciting rhymes and songs with vigorous physical actions such as the 'Hokey Cokey' and 'In and Out the Dusty Bluebells'. Emphasize rhyme and rhythm by sometimes asking the children to tap, clap or stamp their feet, rather than follow the actions.

HOME LINKS
Invite parents to arrive early to collect their children to watch them enjoying their rhymes and songs at the end of a session. Encourage parents to join in and request favourites of their own.

MULTICULTURAL LINKS
Introduce the children to simple songs or rhymes from a wide range of cultures.

GROUP SIZE
Four children.

TIMING
20 minutes.

NUMBER FUN

Learning objective
To recognize numerals 1 to 9. (Mathematical development)

What you need
The photocopiable sheet on page 78; chalk; large numbered cards from 1 to 9; beanbags.

Preparation
If your outdoor surface is not already painted with number patterns such as a hopscotch grid or a snake with numbered sections, then create some outlines and numbers of your own with chalk. Make sure that each number is represented at least four times. Include some numbered stepping-stones, arranged so that it is easy for the children to jump across them in the correct order from 1 to 9.

What to do
Take the children outdoors and let them explore the markings freely. Hold up a number 1 and ask the children if they can find the same number on the ground. How many can they find? Continue to hold up the numbers in order until they have all been named and the children have found them on the ground. Play simple games, for example, ask the children to run around until you hold up a number and then to go and stand on the same number. If a child is already standing on that number then they must search to find a vacant one.

Play games with the beanbags, for example, trying to throw them from one stepping-stone to the next or along the hopscotch grid. Emphasize numerical order from 1 to 9 as you do so.

Allow time for the children to play freely, with and without the beanbags. Have fun jumping across markings such as stepping-stones, the rungs of a ladder or the sections of a snake, from 1 to 9.

Support
Follow the same activities but concentrate on the numbers 1 to 5, until the children can count and recognize these numbers with confidence.

Extension
Introduce the number 10 to older children. Give them a card copy of the photocopiable sheet on page 78 and a small plastic frog. Invite them to make the frog jump across the lily pads in the correct order from 1 to 10.

HOME LINKS
Invite parents to spend time with their children in the outdoor area. Explain the learning objective and ask them to point out numbers in the environment to their children, for example, when shopping.

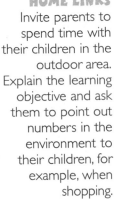

GROUP SIZE
Four children.

TIMING
30 minutes for preparation; ten minutes for main activity.

WHAT SHALL WE WEAR TODAY?

Learning objective

To look closely at similarities, differences, patterns and change. (Knowledge and understanding of the world)

What you need

Large sheets of card; felt-tipped pens; paint; scissors; laminator or sticky-backed plastic; Velcro strips; PVA glue; storage box.

What to do

Ask a child to lie down on a sheet of thick card and draw around him or her. Invite the children to help to paint the outline as if is dressed in indoor clothes. Glue small strips of Velcro to the hands, arms, feet, head, chest, lower abdomen and legs.

Using the outline as a guide, draw some clothing and accessories on card suitable for outdoor play in all types of weather, for example, a sun-hat, sun-glasses, coat, anorak, scarf, woollen hat, gloves and boots. Colour the items with a felt-tipped pen, cut them out, add a label and laminate them or cover in sticky-backed plastic. Peel off the top of the strips of Velcro from the body outline and glue them to the back of the items, cutting out more if there are insufficient. Hang the body outline near to the exit to the outdoor play area, with the caption 'What should we wear when we go outside?'. Put the clothing cards in a box underneath.

Take the children outdoors and talk about the weather conditions. What do they think that they should wear in order to be comfortable as they play? Go back indoors and ask the children to look through the card clothing and choose appropriate items to attach to the displayed body outline. Repeat the activity daily, changing the items if necessary and discussing why changes have been made.

Support

Give younger children samples of real clothing and accessories to handle to support their understanding of the activity.

Extension

Ask older children to put a tick on a weekly chart against pictures of the items chosen for each day. At the end of the week, discuss the clothes worn most frequently and how weather changes affected choices.

HOME LINKS
Ask parents to supply resources for a display on clothing and accessories for different weathers.

MULTICULTURAL LINKS
Include all languages relevant to the children in the group on the clothing labels and include examples of clothing worn by different cultures. Ask parents or bilingual support staff to help, if necessary.

GROUP SIZE
Six children.

TIMING
20 minutes.

HOME LINKS
Explain the learning objective and suggest that parents take children to parks to use large apparatus and develop their awareness of open spaces and of other children playing around them.

INTO ACTION

Learning objective
To show an awareness of space, of themselves and of others. (Physical development)

What you need
A range of large apparatus such as a bench, 'A' frame and tunnel; small mats; hoops; soft-play shapes.

Preparation
Set out the apparatus outdoors, or in a large indoor space, considering the movements that the children will need to make in order to negotiate each piece of equipment. Include opportunities to climb over and under obstacles, crawl through confined spaces and negotiate holes and boundaries. If apparatus is limited, use the other materials that you have available, for example, a rope to balance along, large packing cases to crawl into and a low table draped in a blanket as a tunnel.

What to do
Introduce the children to the apparatus by walking around it without touching it. Stop at intervals and talk about how they might move between the different pieces of equipment, using vocabulary, such as 'over', 'through' 'behind' and 'between'. Follow this by suggesting they try to move on the apparatus themselves, choosing how they will do so. Let them start in different areas so that they have space to move comfortably. Emphasize the need to wait for another child to finish using a piece of apparatus, if necessary. Praise the children for demonstrating this awareness of others around them.

Encourage the children's individual ideas by making positive comments. You might respond to a child hopping between the hoops and then jumping in and out of them by saying, 'I noticed the way that you hopped to this hoop and then jumped into it with both feet together. Well done!'. Always stand where you can observe every child and be aware of potential dangers. Emphasize simple safety rules on larger apparatus, for example, holding handrails on slides and gripping at three points on climbing frames when moving a hand or foot.

Support
Use apparatus such as lower slides and climbing frames for younger children, Provide adult support if the children are anxious.

Extension
Challenge older children by creating an obstacle course with a theme, such as a pirate ship or a jungle.

GROUP SIZE
Up to 12 children.

TIMING
Ten minutes.

STOP, LOOK AND LISTEN

Learning objective
To respond in a variety of ways to what they see, hear, smell, touch and feel. (Creative development)

What you need
Just the children.

What to do
This is an ideal activity to calm children just before coming indoors after vigorous outdoor play, and to raise awareness of their surroundings through their senses. Ask the children to run about and then stand very still on a given signal, such as holding your arms above your head. Once they have done this several times, invite them to continue standing still while they take turns to describe one thing that they can see. Can the others guess the object by the description? Encourage the children to give a detailed description of colour, shape and size.

Now ask the children to listen very carefully to the sounds around them and to talk about specific sounds that they can hear such as traffic or bird-song. They may find concentrating on sound easier if they close their eyes. Are the sounds loud or quiet? Do the things that are making the sounds seem near or far away?

Ask the children to take some big sniffs. Can they smell anything? Try this at different times, perhaps when lunch is being prepared or when someone has a bonfire in a nearby garden.

Explain that the children have been using their eyes, ears and noses to see, hear and smell things and then ask how they touch and taste things. Can the children find something rough to touch without moving from their space? They might feel the ground or a knitted hat. Now can they find something smooth? What about their skin or shiny shoes?

At circle time, include a follow-up discussion about the activity and how useful our five senses can be.

Support
Encourage younger children to point to things, then introduce appropriate vocabulary as they describe them to you.

Extension
Encourage older children to take photographs of the things that they are describing to include in a 'senses' book about their outdoor experiences.

HOME LINKS
Explain the learning objective and encourage parents to talk about what the children see, hear, smell and touch during their walks together.

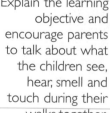

GROUP SIZE
Four children for the activity; two to use the hide with an adult.

TIMING
Fifteen minutes.

FEATHERED FRIENDS

Learning objective
To find out about, and identify, some features of living things, objects and events they observe. (Knowledge and understanding of the world)

What you need
An 'A' frame; old blanket; scissors; two pairs of binoculars; two small chairs; cushion; small table; bird-table; balls of fat; bags of nuts; birdseed; flat dish; information books about birds; paper; paint; felt-tipped pens.

What to do
Take the children outdoors to feed the birds. Give them some fat balls and nut bags to hang up and some seeds to sprinkle on the table. Fill the shallow dish with water. Improvise with a box if you do not have a bird-table but remove this after the activity in case there are cats nearby.

Talk about what would happen if the children stood beside the bird-table to see if the birds came to eat the food. Would the birds come? Why not? Consider that they might be frightened by the children and explain about how farmers put scarecrows in the fields to stop birds eating his seeds. Tell the children how birdwatchers use hides to observe the birds without frightening them. Suggest that the children make their own hide.

Stand the 'A' frame in a quiet place near to the bird-table and cover it in the blanket. Put two small chairs inside, side by side, and cut holes in the blanket large enough for the children to look through when sitting on the chairs. Include a cushion for an adult and a small table with the binoculars on it.

For safety reasons, arrange for an adult to take the children to use the hide two at a time. Choose a quiet time when there are no other children playing outdoors and sit inside the hide. Encourage the children to use the binoculars and compare the features of the birds.

Back indoors, look for the birds that you have seen in books and let the children draw or paint pictures of them.

Support
Younger children will enjoy the excitement of simply looking through the holes in the hide and whispering about what they can see.

Extension
Invite older children to take photographs of the birds that they observe, then make a bird book to share with others.

HOME LINKS
Suggest that parents encourage their children to put out food for the birds at home and to observe them from a distance.

GROUP SIZE
Six children.

TIMING
Ten minutes.

HOME LINKS
Encourage parents to take their children out in different weathers and to share their sensory experiences.

MULTICULTURAL LINKS
Make comparisons between climates in different countries. Invite parents to bring in samples of traditional clothes they would wear in these climates.

RAINY DAYS

Learning objective
To respond in a variety of ways to what they see, hear, smell, touch and feel. (Creative development)

What you need
Outdoor clothing and footwear suitable for a rainy day; umbrellas; small towel; metal pan lid; watering can, if necessary.

What to do
Carry out this activity on a rainy day or, alternatively, create rain showers using a watering can. Observe rain from indoors, watching it run down window frames, splashing on the ground and forming puddles. Talk about memories of being out in the rain. Did the children enjoy the experience?

Get ready to go outside and talk about the choice of clothing and footwear needed. Why do the children wear wellington boots? What would happen if they went out in slippers? Stand outside and encourage the children to talk about their first impressions. Does the rain feel warm or cold? It is soft or hard? Ask them to close their eyes and tilt their heads upwards. Can they feel the rain running down their faces. Suggest they hold their hands out flat. Does the rain splash back out of their open palms or form a little puddle in the centre?

Stand very still and talk about the sounds that the rain is making. Hold out a metal pan lid in one hand and a small towel in the other. Does the rain sound the same on both? Invite the children to take turns to stand under the umbrellas and talk about the noise of the rain over their heads. Let them splash in some puddles and try to make different sounds by jumping or tiptoeing in and out of them.

Talk about the smell of the rain. Can the children think of words to describe it? Does it remind them of anything?

Support
Shorten the activity for very young children who may feel cold quickly. Do not insist on going out if children prefer to watch the rain from indoors.

Extension
Read the rhyme on the photocopiable sheet on page 73. Talk to older children about their sensory experiences related to rain. Create 'rainy pictures' by dropping blobs of paint on to pieces of paper and holding them out in the rain for a few seconds.

GROUP SIZE
Four children.

TIMING
Ten minutes.

HOME LINKS
Send home a leaflet about the dangers of sun exposure and encourage parents to involve their children in their own protection routines.

MULTICULTURAL LINKS
Talk about differences in climate around the world. Discuss the children's experiences of holidays in other countries and talk about how some places have more sunshine than others.

SUNNY ROUTINES

Learning objective
To dress and undress independently and manage their own personal hygiene. (Personal, social and emotional development)

What you need
A sun-hat and sun protection cream for each child; plastic storage boxes.

Preparation
Send home a letter to parents asking them to supply a sun-hat and some sun protection cream for their children. Suggest that they name the hat and label the cream beforehand. Put the hats and creams in separate storage containers.

What to do
Discuss the clothing that children wear in hot weather such as shorts and T-shirts and summer dresses. Compare these with clothes worn in cold or

wet weather. How would the children feel if they went outside on a hot day wearing a coat, hat, scarf and gloves? Would they play in the snow wearing a summer dress?

Show the children the box of sun-hats. Why do they think they are called sun-hats? Talk about the importance of shading their eyes and protecting their heads and necks from the bright sunshine. Pass the hats around and discuss the different shapes. Explain how the wide brims or peaks cast shade over the face and the flaps at the back protect the neck.

Ask the children to look at the different sun protection creams. Have they used them at home? When do their parents apply the creams? Discuss the dangers of the sun's rays and explain how every bit of exposed skin should be protected. Fifteen minutes before going outdoors, ask the children to find their cream in the container and encourage them to apply it, making sure that they cover all exposed skin. Do this as part of your daily routine on sunny days. Just before going out ask the children to find their sun-hats and to put them on.

Support
Younger children will need help in applying the cream. Let them manage simple parts of the routine such as spreading cream on their arms.

Extension
Encourage older children to apply the cream themselves but put it on their faces for them so that they do not sting their eyes.

GROUP SIZE
Six children.

TIMING
20 minutes.

FUN IN THE WIND

Learning objective

To ask questions about why things happen and how things work. (Knowledge and understanding of the world)

What you need

A kite; tissue paper; carrier bags; strong wrapping paper; polythene; thin fabric; dowelling; fretsaw; sticky tape; thin string.

Preparation

Invite parents to bring in examples of different kites and arrange them on a display board and table so that the children can explore them before the activity. Prepare some simple frames using a short and a long piece of dowelling taped together to form a cross shape. Cut slots in the ends of the dowelling and attach thin string between the canes and through the slots to create a kite frame. Cut out pieces of wrapping paper, polythene and fabric slightly larger than the frames.

What to do

Explore the collection of kites and take one outside to fly together. Talk about how the kite moves with the wind. Suggest that the children might make kites of their own.

Give each child a prepared frame and invite them to choose a piece of polythene, fabric or paper. Help them to attach the material to the frame by overlapping the edges and taping it down. Always observe the children closely as they work with polythene and explain the dangers of putting it near their faces. Create a tail for the kite from string with twisted tissue-paper bows and attach a length of string to the point where the pieces of dowelling join.

Run around outside with the kites, holding the end of the string. Which materials prove most successful? Do the kites work when there is no wind? Why not?

Support

Younger children will enjoy making a simple kite from a square of paper with a piece of string attached. Let them decorate the paper with brightly-coloured crayons, then run along holding their kites up in the air.

Extension

Make windmills from folded card with older children and push them in the ground outside. Notice how they increase in speed as the wind blows harder.

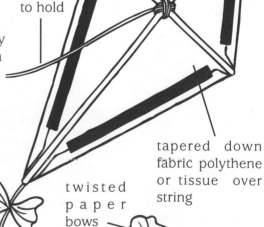

string
to hold

tapered down
fabric polythene
or tissue over
string

twisted
paper
bows

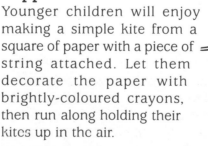

HOME LINKS
Explain the learning objective to parents and send home instructions for making a simple windmill or kite so that they can continue investigations at home with their children.

MULTICULTURAL LINKS
Celebrate the Japanese festival of Kodomono-hi/ Japanese Children's Day (5 May each year) when kites are made in the shape of carp and flown from poles in gardens.

CHAPTER 5

Tidy-up time

Discover how this daily necessity can present new learning opportunities for the children to take responsibility for keeping their own environment tidy, learning how to use tools and discovering that everything has its place.

GROUP SIZE
Six children.

TIMING
Ten minutes.

WHERE DOES IT GO?

Learning objective
To select and use activities and resources independently. (Personal, social and emotional development)

What you need
Drawstring bag; examples of objects from different play areas.

Preparation
Ensure that the contents of storage containers and drawers are easily identifiable by using labels and pictures. Include shadow templates for equipment in sand, water and woodwork areas. Collect one object from each play area, choosing examples that are easily linked to an area such as a paintbrush (art and craft area) or a Duplo brick (construction) and put these objects in a drawstring bag.

What to do
Just before tidy-up time, ask a small group of children to sit in a circle with the bag in the centre. Explain that the bag is full of things that you have found in the wrong place and invite the children to help you to return them to the correct places. Invite one of the children to take an object out of the bag and show it to the others. Can the child say what it is and which play area it is from? Do the other children agree?

Take the object to the suggested play area together and put it back in the correct place, for example, in a storage container or on a shadow template. Discuss how you know where to put it. Once all of the items have been returned to the play areas, ask the rest of the children to join the groups and allocate areas for small groups of children to tidy up.

Once the room is tidy, invite the children to sit down and talk about the things that they picked up or put away. Which areas were the easiest to tidy? Which areas took the longest? Discuss the importance of putting things back after using them.

Support
Encourage younger children to notice the pictures identifying the contents of storage containers and the shadow templates to help them to tidy up.

Extension
Copy the photocopiable sheet on page 79 on to card and cut out the eight pictures. Encourage older children to identify the correct play area location.

HOME LINKS
Encourage parents to involve their children in keeping their toys and personal space at home tidy. Suggest that they make things easier for them by labelling storage containers.

GROUP SIZE
Four children.

TIMING
15 minutes.

LABELS FOR EVERYTHING!

Learning objective

To read a range of familiar and common words and simple sentences independently. (Communication, language and literacy)

What you need

Card; paper; computer; printer; laminator; two identical early years catalogues; glue sticks; scissors.

Preparation

Make a large sign for each play area, for example, 'sand' and 'home area'. Use large clear lettering and laminate the signs for protection. Suspend them above the areas or attach them to screens. Label storage containers to identify the contents. Type and print out labels and find small pictures of the contents in early years catalogues. Glue the label and picture to a small rectangle of card and attach this to the container. Invite the children to choose a picture of something that they like in one of the catalogues, cut it out and glue it to a rectangle of card. Help them to type and print out their names and glue these alongside the picture. Repeat this using the other catalogue so that the same picture can be used. Attach a matching label to each child's personal tray and peg. (For further ideas for using name cards see the activities 'Secret places' on page 18 and 'Name that place' on page 30.)

What to do

Talk to the children about how you have been creating labels to put around the room and ask if they know what a label is. Walk around the room and visit each play area together. Point out the sign above the area and the labels on the storage containers.

Suggest that the children try to read or guess some of the words. Ask them to find their own trays and pegs and discuss how they know which ones are theirs.

Support

Read the words on the labels and signs to younger children and move a finger along the words as you do so.

Extension

Encourage older children to use name cards to help them to write their names on pictures and models.

HOME LINKS
Explain the learning objective and ask parents to read captions and signs to their children in the environment, for example, when going on a journey or at the shops.

MULTICULTURAL LINKS
Create signs for play areas in other languages if necessary. If you have signs explaining learning objectives include other languages on these as well, so that all parents are aware of the potential learning opportunities.

GROUP SIZE
Four children.

TIMING
Ten minutes.

ROOM FOR ONE MORE?

Learning objective
To use developing mathematical ideas and methods to solve practical problems. (Mathematical development)

What you need
Card; small-world cars and people; plastic farm animals and dinosaurs; small trays (seed trays are ideal); sticky-backed plastic; thick black felt-tipped pen.

Preparation
Make some shadow templates to match the small-world equipment. Begin by cutting out pieces of card to fit tightly into the bottom of the trays. Take one piece of card and draw around three small vehicles, then colour the outlines to match the colours of the vehicles. Write the number three alongside with a thick black felt-tipped pen. Protect the card by covering it with sticky-backed plastic and push it back into the bottom of the tray.
Repeat this with other trays, creating outlines for people and animals, varying the number from one to five. Draw around the feet rather than the bodies of more difficult shapes such as dinosaurs.

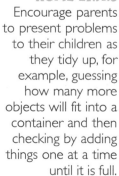

What to do
Explain to the children that you have been making special trays to help them to tidy up their small-world toys. Show them one of the trays and ask them to guess what will fit into it. Demonstrate how to put the equipment on top of the matching outlines. Give each child a tray and ask them to find the correct objects to fit on the outlines. Take turns to count the objects in the trays.

Take the trays to the correct play areas, for example, you might have trays of dinosaurs of different sizes on a table next to the wet sand area or trays of small people next to the water tray. Encourage the children to dry and return the objects to their trays after use.

Support
Concentrate on numbers one to three with younger children, and then gradually introduce four and five.

Extension
Present older children with simple problems using the trays, for example, putting two cars in a tray with four outlines and asking how many more cars are needed to cover all of the outlines.

HOME LINKS
Encourage parents to present problems to their children as they tidy up, for example, guessing how many more objects will fit into a container and then checking by adding things one at a time until it is full.

GROUP SIZE
Four children.

TIMING
20 minutes for the walk; 20 minutes to make the 'litter gobblers'.

THE LITTER GOBBLER

Learning objective
To find out about their environment, and talk about those features they like and dislike. (Knowledge and understanding of the world)

What you need
A large and a small plastic bin; a large and a small cardboard box, suitable for the bins to fit inside; card; recyclable materials; sticky tape; paint; collage scraps; glue.

This is Pol
He likes to g
up litter
Please feed him
your rubbish

What to do
Talk to the children about the importance of disposing of litter properly and take them for a short walk to search for litter bins. Suggest that they use the large box and bin to make a 'litter gobbler' for indoors in the form of an animal character.

Stand the box sideways, put the bin inside and close the flaps at the back. Decide on the type of animal and let the children paint the box an appropriate colour. Help them to draw a face on the front of the box and cut out a large mouth just above the top of the bin

Work with the children to make ears, limbs and feet from coloured card and tape these to the box. Invite the children to suggest other features to add to the 'gobbler' made from recyclable materials such as woollen hair and eyebrows.

Make a sign saying 'This is (choose an appropriate name together). He loves to gobble up litter. Please feed him with your rubbish'. Hang the sign on the front of the box.

Invite the children to deposit rubbish in the 'litter gobbler' by posting it through the open mouth. Empty it by opening the flaps at the back of the box and taking out the bin.

Let the children work together to make a smaller version of the 'litter gobbler' for use in your outdoor area.

Support
Stand the 'litter gobbler' in the art and craft area. Show younger children how to post their leftover scraps of paper into the 'litter gobler' to keep the area tidy.

Extension
Talk to older children about the importance of recycling products and let them design and create their own 'litter gobblers' to accompany the activity 'Bring in your treasure' on page 12.

HOME LINKS
Explain the purpose of the 'litter gobblers'. Ask parents to point out litter bins and encourage their children to use them when they are outdoors.

GROUP SIZE
Four children.

TIMING
Ten minutes.

SWEEP, MOP AND WIPE

Learning objective
To move with control and coordination. (Physical development)

What you need
Squeezy mop or mop and plastic mop-bucket; plastic buckets; brooms with shortened handles; dustpan and brush; cloths; dusters; towels.

What to do
Collect together all of the cleaning tools, put them on the floor and invite the children to sit around them. Take turns to pick up an object, name it and talk about how it can be used. Ask the children which of the objects they would use to clean up spills in the water area. Can they give reasons for their choices? What would they use to sweep up sand or to wipe dough from tables?

Give each child something to carry, and walk around the room together deciding where to leave the objects so that other children can use them to clean the play areas.

At tidy-up time, walk into each play area as the children are tidying and demonstrate how to use the cleaning tools effectively, if necessary. Put plastic buckets into the sand area to deposit sand swept up from the floor. If the children find using a squeezy mop too difficult, give them a small mop and plastic mop-bucket so that they can squeeze excess moisture out of the mop more effectively.

Invite two children to help to wipe tables. Supply them with cloths and bowls filled with warm soapy water and show them how to squeeze the cloths over the bowls to wring out the excess moisture. Why do they think the water is warm and soapy? Would cold water alone clean the table as efficiently? Provide towels for the children to dry their hands.

At circle time, talk about the cleaning tasks that the children have undertaken. Ask individual children to mime their actions and use appropriate vocabulary to describe the physical movements that they make, for example, wringing, wiping, twisting, pushing and shaking.

HOME LINKS
Encourage parents to develop their children's physical skills by asking them to help with tidying and cleaning activities at home such as washing the car, sweeping the path or dusting furniture.

Support
Involve younger children with simple tasks such as dusting the home area and sweeping the dry sand next to the sand tray.

Extension
Invite older children to help with washing up and putting things away after snacks and meals. Encourage them to wash doll's clothes and plastic equipment at regular intervals.

GROUP SIZE
Up to eight children for discussion; one child to make the chosen sound.

TIMING
Ten minutes for discussion; five minutes for activity.

SOUNDS LIKE TIDY-UP TIME

Learning objective
To recognize and explore how sounds can be changed and recognize repeated sounds. (Creative development)

What you need
A selection of sound-making instruments; large sheet of card; thick felt-tipped pen.

Preparation
Create a chart divided into six columns as shown on the diagram. Prepare a name card for each child and cards depicting the instruments available. Attach a strip of Velcro to the back of each card.

This week's tidy-up sound is:	Who will play our tidy-up sound today?				
	Monday	Tuesday	Wednesday	Thursday	Friday
[drum]	▢	▢	Jamie	▢	▢

What to do
Talk to the children about tidying up. How do they know when to start? Suggest that they have a special 'tidy-up' sound and ask them for suggestions. Try out your selection of musical instruments. Do they make quiet or loud noises? Ask some children to go into a play area at the far end of the room and to listen for the different instruments. Did they hear them all? Would it work if a child walked into each play area to make the sound? Consider whether the instruments are easy to carry and play at the same time. Reject any that are heavy, bulky or require two hands to play them.

Suggest that the children choose a different instrument each week as the 'tidy-up' sound. Ask them how they will decide who will play the instrument each day. Do they think that it should it be the same child? Talk about taking turns. How will they know whose turn it is to play the instrument? Show them the chart and cards that you have made and demonstrate how to use them.

At circle time, choose who is to play the instrument and attach a name card to the chart. At tidy-up time, invite the child to walk around the play areas playing the instrument.

Support
Support shy or younger children by walking around with them, or ask them to hold your hand and help you while you play the instrument.

Extension
Encourage older children to think of alternative sounds, for example, carrying around a portable tape recorder playing a favourite song.

HOME LINKS
Suggest that parents explore sound making with their children at home using household objects such as pan lids and wooden spoons.

MULTICULTURAL LINKS
Play instruments related to different festivals, for example, sleigh bells at Christmas or Indian bells during Divali.

GROUP SIZE
Four children.

TIMING
15 minutes.

HOME LINKS
Send home a sheet suggesting appropriate vocabulary for parents to introduce to their children as they make comparisons between the shape and size of objects at home.

LET'S GET SORTED

Learning objective
To use language such as 'circle' or 'bigger' to describe the shape and size of solid and flat shapes. (Mathematical development)

What you need
Card; black felt-tipped pen; scissors; pencil; examples of different shapes and sizes of plastic construction equipment such as Duplo; laminator.

Preparation
Draw around different pieces of construction equipment on to thick card. Colour in the shapes to form a shadow effect. Cut out the card to form smaller, matching cards and laminate them for protection. If the equipment in the play areas is not already displayed on shadows, prepare shadows using this method such as for equipment in the sand and woodwork areas, but do not put them in place yet.

What to do
Spread out the cards depicting shadows of the construction equipment on the floor and leave the pieces of equipment in a pile nearby. Pick up one of the pieces and ask the children to guess which shadow is exactly the same size. Put the piece over the shadow. Were the children correct?

Take turns to place pieces of equipment over the correct shadows. If you already have shadows in place in your play areas, then spend the rest of the time playing freely with the construction equipment and cards, emphasizing vocabulary related to size and shape.

Suggest to the children that shadow cards in play areas would help them to find things and to return them to the correct place while they are playing or tidying up. Show the children one of the prepared shadows with a recognizable shape, for example, a woodwork tool. Can they say which play area it should be in? Continue to look at the shadows and consider where to put them. Talk about the different shapes using appropriate vocabulary such as 'bigger' or 'circle'.

Explain that you are going to attach the shadows to tables and shelves in the play areas ready for the children to use later.

Support
Introduce younger children to words describing simple shapes, such as circle and square, and refer to differences in size.

Extension
Copy the photocopiable sheet on page 80 on to card and cut out the pictures. Invite older children to match the pictures to their shadows and talk about the shapes.

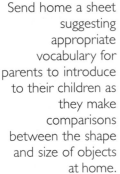

GROUP SIZE
Whole group for discussion; groups of four children for activity.

TIMING
Ten minutes.

HOME LINKS
Suggest that parents encourage their children to concentrate and sit quietly at home, for example, by playing board games with them or completing puzzles together which require close attention.

MULTICULTURAL LINKS
Ensure that the children, for whom English is an additional language, are fully supported so that they understand what is expected of them, and are more able to concentrate and maintain attention as a result.

WAITING FOR THE SIGNAL

Learning objective
To maintain attention, concentrate and sit quietly when appropriate. (Personal, social and emotional development)

What you need
Musical instrument.

What to do
Talk with the whole group about the importance of tidying up carefully and leaving things ready for the next group. Discuss what tidying up involves, for example, picking things up off the floor and putting them back on to shadow templates, or sorting things into labelled storage containers.

Divide the whole group into groups of four children to tidy the play areas, mixing ages so that older children can support younger ones in their task. Explain the reasons for the choice of group members, telling younger children that they can ask their older friends to help them.

Tell the children that you are going to let them know when all of the areas are tidied and discuss suitable ways of attracting their attention, for example, clapping your hands or playing a musical instrument. Ask the children which instrument they think would be the easiest to hear?

Allocate a play area to each group and ask the children to tidy up that area. When the children are satisfied that the area is tidy, suggest that they sit down and wait for the given signal indicating that all of the areas are now tidy. Ask a staff member to praise the children for their efforts and instruct them about what to do next while they remain listening. This activity links to 'Where does it go?' on page 49, where the children tour the play areas after they have been tidied and praise one another for their work.

Support
Ask older children and staff members to help younger children to tidy up and support them as they follow instructions.

Extension
Praise older children for taking responsibility for ensuring that their play area is fully tidy and for supporting younger children.

GROUP SIZE
Four children.

TIMING
Ten minutes.

WHO TIDIED UP HERE TODAY?

Learning objective
To attempt writing for different purposes, using features of different forms, such as lists, stories and instructions. (Communication, language and literacy)

What you need
Paper; clipboards; string; pencils.

Preparation
Prepare sheets of paper to go on the clipboards by writing 'Who has helped to tidy up today?' in clear letters at the top of each sheet. Fasten a sheet to each clipboard and attach a pencil with string. Hang a clipboard in each play area.

What to do
Praise the children for their tidying efforts over the preceding days and explain that you would like to know who was responsible for tidying each area so that you can thank them personally. Discuss with the children how you can find this out.

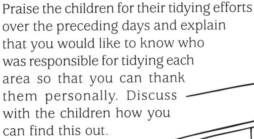

Show the children a prepared clipboard and read the words at the top. Tell them that the clipboard is for them to write down their names when they have finished tidying an area. (This could also be done at the end of the activity 'Waiting for the signal' on page 56.) Emphasize that it does not matter if they cannot write their names yet as they can write their initial letter or make a mark instead.

Allocate areas that are to be tidied and remind the children to make their marks on the clipboard when they have finished. Visit the play areas at the end of the tidying session and ask the children to identify their marks. Praise them for their efforts and replace the sheets ready for the next tidy-up time.

Support
Provide plenty of opportunities for younger children to develop pencil control with free use of writing tools. Praise them for their early efforts and do not insist that they try to form letters before they are ready.

Extension
Involve older children in recording other activities such as hand washing (see 'Splat those germs!' on page 38) or fastening buttons, focusing on specific skills or tasks.

HOME LINKS
Suggest that parents involve their children in mark-making activities at home, for example, writing greetings cards or adding their names or marks to letters.

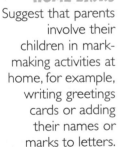

MULTICULTURAL LINKS
Invite the children to bring in stamps from letters that they receive from other countries and use these as a starting point for a discussion on that country.

GROUP SIZE
Two children.

TIMING
Ten minutes.

LET'S WASH UP

Learning objective
To recognize the importance of keeping healthy and those things which contribute to this. (Physical development)

What you need
Two low tables; washing-up brush, bowl and liquid; towel; two aprons; tea towel; cloth; tray; snack foods.

Preparation
Create a simple chart with the caption, 'Who is washing up our snack dishes today?'. Spread a clean towel on a table with a washable surface and put the bowl in the centre. Arrange the tray, aprons and tea towel on a table alongside. Always check for allergies and dietary requirements when choosing foods.

What to do
At circle time, invite two children to help with washing up and display their names on the chart.

While the children are eating their snacks, talk to them about who will be washing up today and discuss why it is necessary to wash dirty dishes. Explain about how germs can make them feel ill and that washing dishes with warm soapy water will remove the germs from them. When the children have finished their snacks, invite a child from each table to collect the cups and put them on the table next to the washing-up bowl. Ask different children to collect any plates or bowls that you have used.

Invite the helpers to put on aprons to protect their clothes. Half-fill the washing-up bowl with warm water and ask one of the children to add a small amount of washing-up liquid. Suggest that one child washes the dishes while the other dries them and puts them on the tray. Show the children how to use the washing-up brush to ensure that all the dishes are fully clean and demonstrate how to put washed dishes upside-down on the towel so that they drain well.

Once the dishes are washed and dried, ask the children to wipe the snack tables using a damp cloth. Show them how to wring the cloth tightly so that they do not make too much mess.

Support
Suggest that a younger child dries the dishes after an older child has washed them.

Extension
Talk to older children about how dishwashers make dishes germ free by rinsing off excess dirt, washing with detergent, rinsing again and then drying with hot air. Make a role-play dishwasher from recyclable materials for the home area.

HOME LINKS
Encourage parents to involve their children in washing dishes at home.

CHAPTER 6

Story time

Enjoy a range of stories and develop the children's literacy skills while focusing on this routine by using props such as puppets and story boxes, and introducing drama and music into the children's experiences of stories.

GROUP SIZE
Up to eight children.

TIMING
15 minutes.

HOME LINKS
Suggest that parents spend time with their children in the story corner looking at the display of books and reading them together.

MULTICULTURAL LINKS
Provide a wide range of stories from many different cultures for the children to look at. Use the stories at the appropriate times throughout the year as you celebrate festivals.

STORIES FROM OTHER CULTURES

Learning objective
To have a developing respect for their own cultures and beliefs and those of other people. (Personal, social and emotional development)

What you need
A selection of stories from other cultures such as *My Granny Went to Market* by Stella Blackstone (Barefoot Books), *Handa's Surprise* by Eileen Browne (Walker Books) and *Oliver's Fruit Salad* by Vivian French (Hodder Children's Books); selection of fruit.

Preparation
Display a selection of story-books from a variety of different cultures in the story corner so that the children can browse through them freely.

What to do
Stimulate initial discussion for your exploration of stories from different cultures by reading books that introduce comparisons between several countries or cultures. Read *My Granny Went to Market* which is a counting rhyme telling the story of a granny's 'round the world' shopping spree on a magic carpet.

Develop the children's knowledge and interest by creating a story sack and interactive display about the book, or make your own book with contributions from the children based on the story.

Follow up this activity by reading *Handa's Surprise* and *Oliver's Fruit Salad* to invite direct comparison between the children's own culture and another, and to develop the children's awareness of cultural differences. Pass around examples of the fruit mentioned in the stories for the children to examine and taste, and make comparisons between Handa and Oliver's clothes, skin and hair. Look at the pictures depicting the environments in which Handa and Oliver live. Ask questions to encourage the children to make comparisons with their own way of life. Would Oliver be likely to see a zebra or elephant walking along beside him? How would Handa feel in a noisy street?

Support
Choose short stories that young children can easily relate to such as *Eat Up, Gemma* by Sarah Hayes (Walker Books).

Extension
Introduce older children to traditional stories associated with different religions, for example the Buddhist story, *Siddhartha and the Swan* by Adiccabandhu and Padmasri (Windhorse Publications).

GROUP SIZE
Six children.

TIMING
Ten minutes.

THAT'S MY FAVOURITE

Learning objective
To retell narratives in the correct sequence, drawing on language patterns of stories. (Communication, language and literacy)

What you need
Card; paint; paper; scissors; glue; frieze paper; table; a selection of books including the children's favourite titles.

Preparation
Choose six of the most frequently-requested story-books and display these on a table. Make small paper representations of the front covers of the books by dividing an A4 sheet of paper into six sections and writing the title of one of the books in each section. Add a simple outline drawing alongside each title. Photocopy the page several times and cut out the six sections. Make a graph by dividing a large sheet of card into six columns, each subdivided into squares. Entitle the graph 'Our favourite story-books'.

What to do
Invite the children to look at the six books and decide which of these they like best. Ask them to select one of the pieces of paper depicting the cover of their favourite book from those that you have prepared and show them how to stick this to the graph in the appropriate column.

Look at the graph together and decide which is the most popular story from the selection available. If two titles have the same number of votes, declare them both winners. Read the winning story/stories together and encourage the children to join in with familiar line endings and word repetition. Encourage the children to recognize the language pattern of the story, for example, by asking them appropriate questions about how the story starts and ends and who the main characters are. Ask for volunteers to retell the story in the correct sequence while the others listen.

Support
Let younger children listen if they prefer to do so but support them in their efforts if they try to retell the story.

Extension
Suggest that older children paint pictures of their favourite part of the chosen story to display around the graph. Ask them to describe what they have painted and write appropriate captions for them. Encourage them to dramatize the story in the correct sequence.

HOME LINKS
Have 'My favourite story' weeks and suggest that parents obtain copies of the stories from the library to read at home.

MULTICULTURAL LINKS
Introduce a wide range of stories representing different cultures from which children can choose their favourites.

GROUP SIZE
Four children.

TIMING
15 minutes.

THE THREE BILLY GOATS GRUFF

Learning objective
To use language such as 'greater', 'smaller', 'heavier' or 'lighter' to compare quantities. (Mathematical development)

What you need
The story of *The Three Billy Goats Gruff* (*First Favourite Tales* series, Ladybird Books); goats of different sizes from a toy farm; toy to represent a troll; wood offcuts; wooden ruler; artificial grass; small boxes; strip of blue foil.

What to do
Read the story with the children, emphasizing the words associated with the comparative size of the goats and the troll. Suggest that the children re-enact the story using the toy goats and troll. Put a pile of toy goats on to the carpet and ask the children to decide which should be the little billy goat. Can they give a reason for their choice? Choose a 'middle-sized' billy goat and a 'great big' billy goat in the same way. Look through the small- world characters to choose a suitably fierce one to represent the troll.

Pile the small boxes at random on the carpet and cover them with the artificial grass, or a piece of green fabric, to represent the meadow. Make a river at the edge of the meadow using a scrunched-up strip of blue foil. Build a bridge from the wood offcuts with the ruler across the top. Hide the 'troll' under the bridge and stand the three goats on the carpet opposite the meadow.

Look at the goats again and talk with the children about the difference between the little, middle-sized and great big billy goats to reinforce the use of appropriate size vocabulary. Point to the troll under the bridge and use words to describe him such as 'fierce', 'heavy' and 'huge'. Invite each child to move one of the characters as the story is told. Emphasize words related to size and weight as you follow the sequence of the story.

Support
Place less emphasis on the description of the troll if younger children find this part of the story frightening. Spend more time playing with the goats, arranging them in order of size and counting them.

Extension
Read other stories related to size such as 'Goldilocks' (Traditional) and 'Jack and the Beanstalk' (Traditional) as well as the stories about *Titch* by Pat Hutchins (Red Fox).

HOME LINKS
Supply parents with suggestions for carrying out activities at home with their children involving size and weight comparisons, for example, using a height chart or making play dough.

GROUP SIZE
Four children.

TIMING
20 minutes.

THE THREE LITTLE PIGS

Learning objective

To build and construct with a wide range of objects, selecting appropriate resources, and adapting their work where necessary. (Knowledge and understanding of the world)

What you need

The story of *The Three Little Pigs* (*First Favourite Tales* series, Ladybird Books); three toy farm pigs; a plastic wolf; straw; sticks; small plastic bricks; string; tape.

What to do

Read the story to the children and talk about how the pigs made their houses. Suggest that they try to build houses using the same materials for three of their toy farmyard pigs.

Put straw in the centre of a table and let the children experiment with building houses. Ask them if they can think of ways of keeping the straw together and show them how farmers used to bundle straw together by tying it in sheaves and propping the sheaves up against one another.

Make a tepee shape using this method and stand it on an empty table with a toy pig inside.

Next, invite the children to try to make a house with sticks. Is it any easier? Encourage the children to try joining the sticks with tape or string in a cone shape so that the leaning sticks support one another. Stand the finished house next to the straw house and put another toy pig inside.

Use the construction equipment to make the 'brick' house, stand it alongside the others and put the third toy pig inside. Can the children say why it was easier to make this house?

As you re-read the story, invite the children to make the voices of the pigs and the wolf. Try using a hairdryer on a cold setting to represent the huffs and puffs of the wolf. Do the houses stand up to this artificial wind?

HOME LINKS
Suggest that parents take their children to observe a building site and talk about how houses are built.

MULTICULTURAL LINKS
Make comparisons between homes in different parts of the world and the materials used to build them.

Support

Younger children will need help to build the houses. Be aware of any children that are disturbed by the story, and if necessary, do not make the wolf appear too fierce. Allow the pigs to escape into the next house rather than be eaten by the wolf.

Extension

Encourage older children to make houses from other materials such as clay, wet sand and card and to decide which are the strongest.

GROUP SIZE
Six children.

TIMING
20 minutes.

GOING ON A JOURNEY

Learning objective
To travel around, under, over and through balancing and climbing equipment. (Physical development)

What you need
The book *Room on the Broom* by Julia Donaldson (Macmillan Children's Books); bench; broomstick; twigs; strong string; tape; witch's hat; wand; hair clip with bow attached; black plastic cauldron (used to house plants and obtainable from garden centres); brightly-coloured blanket and cushions; selection of large apparatus.

Preparation
Fasten the twigs tightly to the end of the broomstick to form a witch's besom and attach it to the back of the bench with tape.

What to do
Read the story to the children and suggest that they re-enact the story. If this book is not available, adapt the activity to other stories involving a journey such as *We're Going on a Bear Hunt* by Michael Rosen (Walker Books) or *Rosie's Walk* by Pat Hutchins (Red Fox).

Invite two children to play the part of the witch and her cat and ask them to climb on to the broomstick. Make sure that the witch is wearing her hat and bow and carrying her wand. Stand the cauldron on the back of the bench. As you read the story, talk about how the witch and her cat will move astride the broomstick. Encourage them to hang on tightly and bend backwards and forwards in the wind with the witch wailing and the cat hissing.

Ask the other children to play the part of the animals, hiding under and behind the apparatus ready to pick up the things that the witch drops. Every time something is dropped, the witch and her cat should leave the broom and search around, over and under apparatus. One at a time, the animals should find the items and join the witch on her broom until, finally, the broom snaps. Encourage the children to pretend to fall through the air. Invite a child to be a fierce dragon and suggest that the other children yowl and growl and scare him away. Put a bright blanket and cushions over the bench so that it can be transformed into a 'truly magnificent broom' with the witch's spell.

HOME LINKS
Encourage parents to take their children to the park to play on large apparatus and to act out other stories that they have enjoyed.

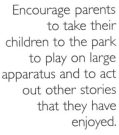

Support
Let younger children just play on the broomstick, bench and apparatus.

Extension
Invite parents to watch older children act out the story.

GROUP SIZE
Four children.

TIMING
20 minutes.

SIMPLE PUPPETRY

Learning objective
To use their imagination in art and design, music and stories. (Creative development)

What you need
Story-books; glove and finger puppets; dolls and soft toys; wooden spoons; elastic bands; scraps of fabric; scissors; felt-tipped pens; glue; wool; small collage items such as sequins and buttons; a playhouse with a window or a three-sided clothes horse; curtains.

Preparation
Create a puppet theatre from a playhouse, using the window space to display the puppets, or drape a three-sided clothes horse in curtains leaving a gap in the centre.

What to do
Read some of the children's favourite stories to them using glove and finger puppets, dolls or soft toys as the characters. Suggest that the children make some special puppets of their own so that they can dramatize their favourite stories.

Choose a popular story with a few distinctive characters such as 'Little Red Riding Hood' (*First Favourite Tales* series, Ladybird Books). Read the story together and make a list of the characters that you will need to create. Give the children a wooden spoon each and decide which character they will make. Show them how to paint the bowl of the spoon and part of the handle in an appropriate colour to represent skin or the coat of an animal. Let them create facial features from small collage scraps such as sequins, buttons and pieces of fabric, and glue on some woollen hair. Help the children to cut out a circle of fabric with a hole in the centre and to thread the spoon handle through the hole. Secure the fabric with an elastic band around the top of the handle so that the child's hand is hidden underneath when the puppet is operated.

Show the children the puppet theatre and demonstrate how to kneel or sit behind it to operate the puppets. Let the children play freely with the theatre and puppets to re-enact stories or make up some of their own.

Support
Make the puppets for younger children and play with them together before withdrawing and leaving them to enjoy free play.

Extension
Encourage older children to put on their own performances for younger children and friends to watch at story time.

HOME LINKS
Send home instructions for making a wooden spoon puppet so that parents can share the fun of puppet drama with their children.

MULTICULTURAL LINKS

Use puppets to re-enact stories during religious festivals such as Chinese New Year and Christmas.

GROUP SIZE
Four children.

TIMING
20 minutes to make up the stories; 20 minutes to create the books.

HOME-MADE BOOKS

Learning objective
To use information and communication technology to support their learning. (Knowledge and understanding of the world)

What you need
Small-world equipment such as vehicles, people and animals; play mats; computer; printer; sugar paper; felt-tipped pens; clipboard; paper; glue.

What to do
Allow time at the start of the activity for the children to play freely with the small-world equipment before joining in with their play. Ask each of the children to tell you a story about what is happening with the items and characters that they are playing with. Tell them that you think their stories are really interesting and that the other children might like to hear them at story time.

Working with one child at a time, say that you are going to write the story on your clipboard. As the other children continue to play with the equipment, take the child to the computer and type out a short version of the story, with the main points in separate sentences. Print out the story together. Once all of the stories have been typed and printed take the children to a table and help them to cut the text into separate sentences and glue them on to separate sheets of paper. Join the sheets together to form a book and use sugar paper to make a cover. Invite the children to draw pictures to illustrate their stories.

Hang up the book in the story corner and ask the writers to 'read' their stories to their friends.

Support
Encourage younger children to draw a picture of the things that they played with and type a sentence for them to describe the action in the picture. Put several children's pictures together to form a book.

Extension
Involve older children in operating the computer and printer. Show them which keys to press to indicate choices, for example, the size and colour of lettering, and which buttons are needed to switch the machines on and off.

HOME LINKS

Encourage parents to use computers at home (if they have them) to type family letters and to look up information with their children.

MULTICULTURAL LINKS

Use computers to make books about festivals and events related to other cultures and type out captions. Invite parents to contribute photographs if they are able.

GROUP SIZE
Four children.

TIMING
20 minutes.

THE LITTLE RED HEN

Learning objective

To work as part of a group, taking turns and sharing fairly, understanding that there needs to be agreed values and codes of behaviour for groups of people, including adults and children, to work together harmoniously. (Personal, social and emotional development)

What you need

The story of *The Little Red Hen* (*First Favourite Tales* series, Ladybird Books); grain; small watering can; trowel; small bag of flour; bowl; wooden spoon; salt-dough loaf; plastic bricks in a storage container.

What to do

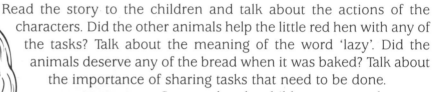

Read the story to the children and talk about the actions of the characters. Did the other animals help the little red hen with any of the tasks? Talk about the meaning of the word 'lazy'. Did the animals deserve any of the bread when it was baked? Talk about the importance of sharing tasks that need to be done.

Suggest that the children re-enact the story, emphasizing that they will need to take turns to speak and that they must listen carefully while someone else is speaking. Decide together who will play the parts of the hen, cat, rat and pig.

Read the story and encourage the children to join in with appropriate lines such as 'Not I' and 'I will'. Introduce the props for added realism.

Ask the children to consider the play areas that they have visited during the session. Did they play alone or with friends? Tip out the plastic bricks and choose one of the children to put them back into the container while the others watch. When the child has put half of the bricks back, invite the rest of the children to help. Was it easier when everyone helped? Suggest that the children work in pairs to help each other to build towers with the bricks, if possible, pairing an older child with a younger one.

Support

Emphasize the importance of helping each other to pick up toys from the floor during tidy-up time.

Extension

Provide wheeled apparatus that encourages co-operation, for example, tricycles with two seats or trolleys. Play simple team games with small apparatus such as throwing beanbags into hoops.

HOME LINKS
Explain the learning objective of working together co-operatively and suggest that parents invite the children's friends to join them for activities such as baking and picnics.

GROUP SIZE
Six children.

TIMING
20 minutes.

HOME LINKS
Send home copies of stories related to festivals and celebrations so that parents can share them with their children.

MULTICULTURAL LINKS
Encourage parents from different cultures to come in and tell traditional stories associated with festivals.

THE STORY OF HOLI

Learning objective

To understand that people have different needs, views, cultures and beliefs, that need to be treated with respect. (Personal, social and emotional development)

What you need

The photocopiable sheet on page 69; five large yoghurt tubs; red, yellow, green, blue and brown coloured tissue paper; tape of Indian dance music; tape recorder; cardboard tube; saris or lengths of fabric; washing line.

Preparation

Ask the children to cut or tear the tissue paper into small pieces, putting each colour into a different yoghurt pot. Make a flute from a cardboard tube by cutting holes along it. Fasten a washing line across the story corner at a safe height.

What to do

Explain the meaning of the word 'festival' and how a lot of stories tell us about the origins of festivals and celebrations. Remind the children of stories that they have already heard of, for example, the animal race that determined the names of the Chinese years.

Read 'The story of Holi' on the photocopiable sheet and explain how it links to the festival. Invite the children to close their eyes and to listen to the music, imagining the milkmaids swaying in time to the music. Suggest that you act out the story using small pieces of coloured tissue paper. Explain that real powder paint would be too messy in the story corner.

Invite two children to be Krishna and Radha and encourage the others to play the parts of milkmaids. Put a pile of yoghurt pots on the floor for Krishna to pretend to break, and suggest that he drapes the saris across the washing line after he has 'broken' them. Play the music for a few minutes so that the milkmaids can dance and Krishna can pretend to play his flute. Have fun throwing the tissue scraps at one another.

Finally, play a game to encourage the children to pick up the tissue scraps, and use them later for collage pictures about Holi.

Support

Younger children will find it easier to tear the tissue rather than cut it.

Extension

Encourage older children to have fun throwing powder paint at large paper outlines of Krishna and Radha spread out on the floor.

GROUP SIZE
Six children.

GROUP SIZE
Six children.

TIMING
Ten minutes.

ONCE UPON A TIME

Learning objective
To extend their vocabulary, exploring the meanings and sounds of new words. (Communication, language and literacy)

What you need
The photocopiable sheet on page 70; examples of fiction and non-fiction library books; tape recorder; blank tape; paper; coloured felt-tipped pens.

What to do
Look at the library books together and ask the children about their experiences of library visits. What kind of books do they like to borrow? Do they sometimes borrow books that help them to learn more about something that they are interested in? Can they give examples? What kind of stories do they like best? Do they have a favourite character? Ask them to look through the books and sort them into two piles: story-books and books that 'tell us more about something' (information books).

Read 'Jamie's story' on the photocopiable sheet. What kind of books did Jamie and his dad enjoy? Re-read the story that Jamie wrote. Emphasize the phrases 'Once upon a time...' and '...happily ever after', and talk about how they often start and finish a story, particularly the fairy-tales that Jamie enjoyed. Talk about how Jamie has used his favourite story about the enormous turnip to give him the idea of the gigantic carrot. Invite the children to think of other variations on this theme such as 'the monstrous cabbage' or the 'huge marrow'. Jamie made the giant in his story friendly and helpful. Do the children prefer friendly giants or do they enjoy the excitement of reading about a fierce ogre?

Suggest that the children think of stories of their own and make recordings of them on a tape. Write these stories for the children and ask them to illustrate them. Make them into simple books and display them alongside a caption 'We made up these stories using words and ideas from our favourite books'.

Support
Read lots of simple stories with younger children to introduce them to new words rather than ask them to make up their own stories.

Extension
Introduce older children to stories that are rich in new vocabulary, rhyme and nonsense sounds.

HOME LINKS
Send home a copy of the photocopiable sheet for parents to read with their children. Suggest that they write down their children's own stories for them to illustrate. Encourage families to visit the library regularly together.

The story of Holi

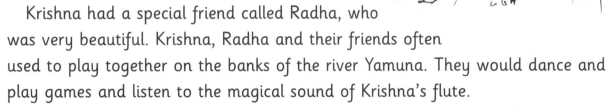

A long time ago in India, there lived a boy called Lord Krishna. He was called 'Lord Krishna' because he was holy and had special powers. Krishna was full of mischief and liked to play tricks on his friends. As he got older he played more and more tricks. Once he broke the milkmaids' pots and another time he took all their clothes away while they were bathing in the river. He hung them in some nearby trees while he played his flute.

Krishna had a special friend called Radha, who was very beautiful. Krishna, Radha and their friends often used to play together on the banks of the river Yamuna. They would dance and play games and listen to the magical sound of Krishna's flute.

One night in early spring, when there was a full moon high in the sky, the milkmaids came out to dance. They wore brightly-coloured clothes that shone as they danced. Radha sang and the milkmaids whirled around to the music of Krishna's flute. People came out of their houses to join in.

Suddenly, Krishna stopped playing and disappeared. He came back a few minutes later with some pots, each one containing a different-coloured powder. He put the pots on the ground and called to Radha. When she got nearer to him he threw a handful of red powder at her, then some yellow and then some green.

Radha shrieked in surprise and everyone stopped dancing. Her face, arms and clothes were red, yellow and green! Quickly, she picked up a pot of blue and a pot of brown powder and threw handfuls back at Krishna.

All of their friends were laughing and some of them started to throw the powder as well. Soon they were all throwing powder at one another. The air became a cloud of colour.

Since then, Holi has been celebrated in early spring. It is a time when people throw coloured powder or paint at one another to remind themselves of the fun Krishna and his friends had on the banks of the river.

Jean Evans

Jamie's story

Jamie loved to read stories. Every Friday, Jamie's dad would take him to the big library in the high street to choose some books to read at bedtime. Jamie and his dad loved to pretend that they were the enormous giants, brave princes, tiny mice or even tall giraffes that they read about in their library books.

One Friday, Dad came to find Jamie. 'Sorry, Jamie,' he said. 'No books tonight. The library has been flooded. It will be closed for at least a week.'

That night, Jamie did not want to go to bed. No library books meant no new adventures to share with Dad! Mum popped her head around the door, 'You know what I would do, Jamie?' she smiled. 'I would write my own story.'

She went back downstairs and found a pen and some paper. 'Tell me your story and I will write it down for you. Then you will still have an adventure to share with Dad.'

'My favourite story is 'The Enormous Turnip', but I like 'Jack and the Beanstalk' as well,' said Jamie with excitement.

'Well, why don't you make up a story that reminds you of both?' asked Mum.

And this is what Mum wrote down for Jamie:

'The gigantic carrot'

by Jamie Brown

Once upon a time a boy called Jamie planted a carrot seed. It grew and grew until it was gigantic. Jamie tried to pull up the gigantic carrot but he only fell backwards. His mum tried to help, and his dad, and his gran, and his sister, but the carrot stayed tightly in the soil. So Jamie climbed a beanstalk to find the giant who lived at the top. 'Will you help me to pull up my carrot?' he asked. The giant climbed down the beanstalk with Jamie on his back. He put one enormous hand around the carrot's leaves and 'pop', up came the carrot. Everyone had carrot soup for tea and lived happily ever after.

Later that night when Dad came into Jamie's bedroom, there was a piece of paper waiting for him. 'Read it, Dad,' said Jamie.

Dad began, 'Once upon a ....'

At the end, he laughed and laughed. 'Well done, Jamie. We didn't need our library books after all!'

Jean Evans

Meet my friends

Sue is a very handy friend,
She makes models with boxes and glue,
Sometimes her towers are taller than me,
Have you got a friend like Sue?

Ross is sometimes an angry friend,
He shouts and stamps when he's cross,
But when he's happy he has a great big smile,
Have you got a friend like Ross?

Naseem is a very cuddly friend,
She likes to sit and dream,
Sometimes she reads a story to me,
Have you got a friend like Naseem?

Jake is a very useful friend,
He knows how to make a cake,
And he always keeps a piece for me,
Have you got a friend like Jake?

Now tell me about your special friends,
And the things that you like to play,
What do you all like doing,
At (name of nursery) every day?

Jean Evans

All about five

Five railway engines,
Chugging down the track,
Along came *(name of child)*,
And put one back.

Five wooden railway lines,
Joined to make a track,
(Name of child) took a piece away,
And put it in the sack.

Five wooden railway lines,
All inside a sack,
(Name of child) took a piece out,
And started to make a track.

Five railway engines,
All inside a sack,
(Name of child) took one out,
And put it on the track.

Jean Evans

Join five pieces of wooden railway track together and put five engines along it. Invite five children to say the rhyme and put an engine into a sack. Repeat with 4, 3, 2 and 1 engine until the track is empty.

Once all the engines are in the sack, continue the rhyme until all the pieces of track have been put into the sack in the same way as above.
The rhyme can then be reversed as follows.

Ask five children to take the pieces of wooden railway track out of the sack 'one by one' as they say the rhyme and to join the track together again.

Invite the children to continue to remove railway engines from the sack 'one by one' and place them on the track as they say the rhyme.

Sensing rain

Come over and look through the window,
A rain shower has just begun,
Put on your boots and your waterproof coats,
And go out and have some fun.

Use your eyes to see the rain,
As it sparkles and drips to the ground,
Search for drops that are shiny and thin,
Or tiny and silver and round.

Move your bodies to feel the rain,
Catch drops that are cold, sharp and prickly,
Or tilt your faces and close your eyes,
To feel streams running warm, soft and tickly.

Use your ears to hear the rain,
Splish, splash as drops bounce to the ground,
Landing in puddles with big loud plops,
Or on walls with a soft drumming sound.

Wrinkle your noses to smell the rain,
Sniff the dampness that hangs in the air,
On leaves, and hedges and warm wet soil,
Soaking clothes and tight curly hair.

What fun and excitement a shower can bring,
A time to learn more about rain,
Now take off your boots and your waterproof coats,
For the sun has come out again!

Jean Evans

Whose special day?
(Tune: 'London Bridge is Falling Down')

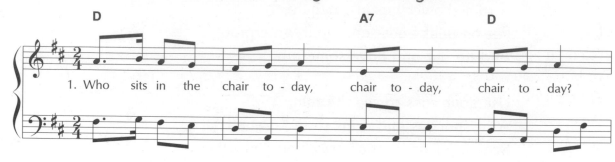

1. Who sits in the chair to-day, chair to-day, chair to-day?

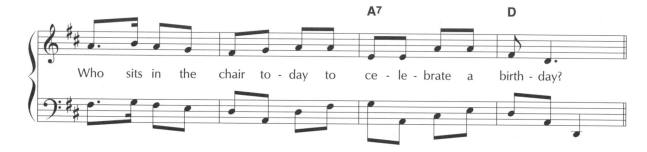

Who sits in the chair to-day to ce-le-brate a birth-day?

(Name of child) sits in the chair today,
Chair today, chair today,
(Name of child) sits in the chair today,
To celebrate his/her birthday.
(child comes out and sits in birthday chair)

Let us give him/her *(age)* loud claps,
(age) loud claps, *(age)* loud claps,
Let us give him/her *(age)* loud claps,
To celebrate his/her birthday.
(clap appropriate number for child's age)

Let's all sing his/her favourite song,
Favourite song, favourite song,
Let's all sing his/her favourite song,
To celebrate his/her birthday.
(all sing song chosen by child)

Jean Evans

Welcome to our library

Dear Parents

> Welcome to our library,
> We hope you'll take a look,
> When picking up your children,
> Please help them choose a book.

Our library

We have organized a library for your children so that you can share their delight as they discover the world of books. We hope that you will take advantage of this and enjoy borrowing books regularly. Why not visit a local library, too, so that your children can look at an even wider selection of books. Let us know if you have any suggestions for new books for our library.

Enjoying books

As parents, encourage your children to develop an awareness of what reading is about, and how much pleasure books and stories can bring to them.

■ Short stories – Children love short story times at any time of the day, but particularly at bedtime. Find somewhere comfortable to sit and invite a favourite soft toy to listen. Be prepared to read the same story several times. Children gain great satisfaction from the security of knowing 'what comes next' and develop an awareness of the rhythm of words as they listen.

■ Telling stories – Younger children love to feel that they are involved with storytelling, so try choosing stories with plenty of repetition, pausing to let your child finish off the repeated lines. With very young children, use books that involve actions such as lifting flaps or pressing buttons.

■ Repeating rhymes – All children love repeating rhymes so remember to include traditional nursery rhymes. These are part of our children's heritage and have lasting appeal.

■ Learning words – As older children become more familiar with books, they will begin to notice the print on the page as well as the illustrations. Point out words and letters and move your finger across the page as you read.

■ Caring for books – Show your children how to handle books with care and respect, and to turn pages in the correct direction. Explain any of the words that are difficult to understand and talk about the author and title of the book.

■ Finding out – Children will be fascinated with well-illustrated information books related to their world or our current topic. Remember that staff will be happy to advise you on appropriate titles at any time.

Making pizzas

The children have thoroughly enjoyed making pizza, so why not try making some at home? Encourage your child to help with weighing, preparing and mixing the ingredients.

For the home-made tomato sauce you will need:
1 small tin of tomatoes
1 small onion
1 dessertspoon of tomato purée

What to do
Peel the onion, chop it and put it in a saucepan. Mix in the tomatoes and tomato purée and cook the sauce for approximately 15 minutes on a low hob, stirring occasionally to prevent it sticking.

For the pizza base you will need:
150g self-raising flour
40g butter or soft margarine
50g cheese
4 tablespoons of milk
Topping suggestions:
Sliced peppers, strips of ham, small sausages, chopped mushrooms, tinned sweetcorn, pineapple chunks, grated cheese, olives, as well as your own ideas.

What to do
■ Weigh out the flour and put it in a mixing bowl along with the butter, chopped into small pieces. Rub the butter and flour together until you have created a fine breadcrumb consistency.
■ Grate the cheese, add it to the mixture and then stir in the milk. Mix all of the ingredients together to form a ball of dough.
■ Divide the mixture in half and roll out one of the pieces into a circle. Repeat with the other half of the mixture and put the two pizza bases on a baking tray.
■ Spread the home-made tomato sauce on to the top of each pizza and give your child a free choice of toppings.
■ Bake the pizzas in the oven for 15 minutes at 220°C/425°F/Gas Mark 7 or until the edges are brown.

Can you set the table?

Help your child to cut around the outlines at the bottom of the page and stick them over the correct shapes to complete the place setting. Ask them to draw their favourite meal on the plate and a drink in the glass.

Across the lily pads

Can you help the frog across the pond? Start on number 1 and count as you go.

Our play areas

Shadow matching